TARGET
Listening and Understanding in Primary Schools

TARGET
Listening and Understanding in Primary Schools

Essential Reading for Effective Learning

For Class Teachers, SENCOs and Support for Learning Staff

Jeanne Reilly
and Sarah Murray

Barrington Stoke
Helen Arkell Dyslexia Centre

First published 2004 in Great Britain by Barrington Stoke Ltd,
Sandeman House, Trunk's Close, 55 High Street, Edinburgh, EH1 1SR

www.barringtonstoke.co.uk

Copyright © 2004 Jeanne Reilly and Sarah Murray

The moral right of the author has been asserted in accordance with the
Copyright, Designs and Patents Act 1988

ISBN 1-84299-158-2

Edited by Julia Rowlandson

Designed and typeset by GreenGate Publishing Services, Tonbridge
Printed in Hong Kong by Sino Publishing House Ltd

Contents

Introduction	1
Checklists	9
The Ideal Teacher	22
The Ideal Classroom	23
1 Listening and Attention	24
2 Phonological Awareness	39
3 Memory	60
4 Vocabulary and Concepts	78
5 Understanding	94
6 Communication	114
Glossary	140
References	143
Useful Resources and Suppliers	144
Index	146
Acknowledgements	149

Introduction

Listening and understanding are vital skills for learning, communicating and making friends. Children are expected to listen and understand throughout the school day. Talking is a major part of most teaching, even though the school curriculum is delivered in many different ways.

The aim of the book

The aim of this book is to help class teachers and learning support assistants to understand and help children who have specific difficulties in 'Listening and Understanding'.

The book will give practical ideas for the classroom that can be used with children who experience problems. Other children in the class are also likely to benefit from these ideas which allow for different learning styles.

Listening and understanding in the classroom

During the school day, children listen to the teacher, one another, sounds and noises in the environment. They make decisions about what to listen to. They judge if they have understood what they have heard.

Should they listen to the teacher telling them something new or should they listen to the child behind asking a question in a whisper? Have they understood the instruction for their maths homework?

Difficulties in either listening or understanding will make it harder for children to access the curriculum.

Making friends

Listening and understanding are also important skills for making friends. As well as understanding the words and nuances of conversation, children listen so they know when and how to join in. Children listen to what they themselves are saying. If other people appear confused, they change what they have said to make it more understandable.

Difficulties with listening and understanding

Many children are already good at listening and understanding when they start school. They will know they must look at the teacher when she tells them to listen. They will understand what she is saying.

However, some children do not seem to listen as well as the rest of the class. They do not understand all that is said to them, although *they* might not be aware of this fact. They are not 'tuned in' to what is going on in the class so do not anticipate what is going to happen next. Often they do not have such good memories as other children.

These children can be more difficult to engage and teach. They may find it harder to learn what the rest of the group grasp easily. It is with these children in mind that this book has been written.

Footnote: For simplicity the teacher will be referred to as 'she' and the child as 'he'.

The children this book can help

The book is intended to describe rather than diagnose children's behaviour and then to offer ideas to help improve their listening and understanding.

Most of the children this book can help will not have a diagnosis of any specific kind. They will be the children the teacher or assistant feel are having difficulty in some aspect of listening and understanding.

There will be *some* children, however, who have been diagnosed with a 'specific learning difficulty'. This might be described as any of the following: Specific Developmental Language Disorder, Dyslexia, Attention Deficit (Hyperactivity) Disorder, Dyspraxia, Autistic Spectrum Disorder, Asperger's Syndrome.

Whether or not there is a diagnosis, they will have a problem in one or more of the six areas described in this book.

How to use this book

We recommend that you start by using the checklists. This will give you a description of what the child can do and identify any areas of need.

The checklists will guide you to the relevant chapters. Each chapter describes a skill area in greater detail. Here you will find general strategies for the teacher and child to use. These strategies are practical tools for use throughout the school day – including assembly, play and lunch times.

Each chapter also includes activities for teachers and assistants to use with the child for more specific work. These can be used with a child of any age and cover a range of skills.

The target cards at the end of each chapter are for the child's use. They will also act as a reminder to the staff in the classroom. Each target card has a specific focus so that the learning is consolidated and transferred.

The child will be helped most if the chapter is followed from the beginning to end. Start by incorporating the general strategies into the daily routine. Teach specific skills using the practical activities. Lastly, introduce the target cards.

A note of caution – build up your use of strategies slowly. This will prevent you and the child becoming overwhelmed. Even the use of one strategy, if this is consistent, will make a difference.

Areas involved in listening and understanding

There are six skill areas which underpin Listening and Understanding. Each is covered in a separate chapter.

1. Through the process of **listening** and **attention** the child focuses on and takes in information.

2. **Phonological awareness** is a very specific kind of listening. It involves focusing on the sounds that make up the words of our language.

3. We sort and store information using our **memory**. Remembering is fundamental to making sense of what is said.

4. **Vocabulary** and **concepts** are important building blocks for language. They provide a mental dictionary to help Listening and Understanding.

5. **Understanding** is the process by which a listener makes sense of what is said. Good understanding of language is vital for learning and thinking.

6 All these skills contribute to effective **communication**. Communication is a social as well as a language based activity. It enables us to make friends, share ideas and learn in a group.

All six skill areas develop alongside each other as part of an interacting system.

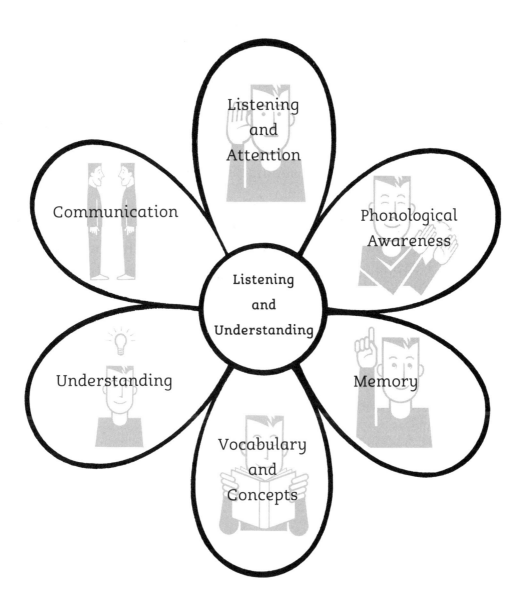

Difficulties in any one area will have repercussions for other aspects of Listening and Understanding. Likewise, progress in any one area will strengthen the system as a whole.

Themes throughout the book

Learning is a process of constant discovery on the part of both child and teacher. Effective teaching involves listening and understanding. It requires listening to what the child is saying and understanding when a change of teaching approach is needed.

Awareness of how he learns best is the most important discovery a child can make. The teacher enables this discovery to be made.

Asking the child to talk about **how** he went about a task leads him to find out whether he learns best by doing (kinaesthetic), seeing (visual), or hearing (auditory).

Asking him **what** he hopes to learn engages the child in his own learning. Asking him **what** he has learnt tells the teacher how effective her teaching has been.

Top tips

Using these top tips will make a real difference to your teaching and the child's learning:

- Support what you say with something the child can see, such as pictures, a demonstration and written words.

- Teach the child to see what you say. Making 'pictures in the head' to help listening and understanding is called *visualisation*.

- Make the routine predictable to reduce the demands on listening and understanding. Be aware that unstructured times like 'break time' can be anything but a break, and may present greater challenges than learning in the classroom.

- Recognise the amount of effort and energy the child uses in order to listen and understand. The child will need to give greater effort to do things which other children find easy.

Quotes from Children

'Sometimes my words are a bit wobbly.'

'My brain's full.'

'When you said the sentence I forgot it straight away.'

'My pen's run out of oil.'

'I know it but I can't remember its name right now.'

'You've got a golden heart (heart of gold).'

'I didn't know there was a name for it. I thought you could just call it anything.'

'Things are a bit more understanding now.'

'Mavilla... vamilla... white ice cream.'

'I'll have to write that down or I'll never remember.'

'My mum tried to explain. I just said yeah yeah yeah. But I didn't really understand.'

Checklists

Identifying what the child can do

*'It isn't that they can't see the solution.
It is that they can't see the problem.'*
G K Chesterton

The aim of the checklists is to help you identify the child's difficulties and guide you towards the strategies and activities which will help him learn best.

Deciding which checklists to use

You may wish to focus on just one checklist or all six. For some children you will already have an idea of the area which is affecting their learning most. For other children you may not yet be sure.

Remember that all six areas overlap. A child who does not understand well may not listen attentively. A child with a poor memory may find it difficult to learn new vocabulary.

We suggest that you read the case studies to help decide which checklists to use. It is recommended that you complete all the checklists for children whose difficulties are not straightforward or easy to pinpoint.

How to use the checklists

- The checklists start with what the child **can** do. This is the best guide to deciding what the child can be helped to do next.
- Each checklist is divided into three age groups (5 to 7 years, 7 to 9 years, 9 to 11 years). Use the part of the checklist which matches the child's age.
- Tick those behaviours which the child can do consistently. Children who do not achieve ticks for **all** the behaviours on the checklist will have a difficulty in that area.
- When you have identified the areas in which the child has difficulties, find the chapter with the corresponding title. There you will find general strategies for helping the child learn in class as well as activities for developing particular skills.
- You may wish to revisit the checklists at a later date. By filling them in again you will be able to measure the child's progress over time.

Case Study – Listening and Attention

Robbie is 9 years old. He needs quick changes between activities to hold his interest and often abandons activities he finds challenging. Robbie is easily distracted. He responds to sounds and movements which the other children ignore. Robbie is also distracted by his own thoughts and complains of being too hot, too tired and hungry. Robbie finds waiting difficult. He often interrupts and sometimes does reckless or dangerous things. Robbie is an enthusiastic and fun-loving boy. He does not appear to be aware of his difficulties.

Listening and Attention Checklist

Name: _____ Date of Birth: _____	
5 TO 7 YEARS	TICK
Listens to a short story in a group situation.	
Continues an activity while listening to simple instructions (e.g. 'finish the colouring and then cut out the shapes').	
Gets started and keeps on task without help.	
7 TO 9 YEARS	
Follows instructions while doing another activity.	
Focuses on an activity, ignoring noises and distractions, such as other children's talk.	
Takes turns and waits in conversation.	
9 TO 11 YEARS	
Listens carefully during class discussions, making contributions and asking questions which take account of other people's ideas and views.	
Takes responsibility for own listening and uses appropriate 'listening strategies', e.g. sits near the front, looks at the speaker.	
Sticks to the topic being discussed.	

Case Study – Phonological Awareness

Megan is 6 years old and can only just write her name. Megan has learnt some letter-sounds and recognises a few words by sight. Megan has a history of hearing and speech difficulties. It can be difficult to follow what she is saying. Her speech sounds 'slurred' and she sometimes gets sounds in the wrong order. Megan is imaginative with a lively sense of humour. The other children find Megan's antics amusing.

Phonological Awareness Checklist

Name: _____ Date of Birth: _____	
5 TO 7 YEARS	*TICK*
Intelligible in most contexts (immaturities with 'r', 'th' and complex blends, e.g. 'str', may persist).	
Splits words into syllables (e.g. *el-e-phant*), initial sound (e.g. *bat* – 'b') and rhyme (e.g. *bat* – 'b-at').	
Splits blends into two sounds (e.g. *spoon* – 's-p').	
Blends three sounds into a simple word (e.g. 'b-a-t – bat').	
7 TO 9 YEARS	
Fully intelligible. All speech sounds used.	
Orders sounds appropriately in spoken words (e.g. *hospital, animal, spaghetti*).	
'Hears' individual sounds within words (e.g. 'p' in *caterpillar*).	
Creates poems based on rhyme (e.g. the frog on the log) and alliteration (e.g. hungry hippos having ham).	
9 TO 11 YEARS	
Understands and uses prefixes and suffixes (e.g. *un*happy, happi*ly*).	
Identifies or invents words where meaning is represented by sound (e.g. *hiss, buzz, bang*).	
'Hears' and understands differences between words with similar sound (e.g. cinnamon/synonym, imperial/interior).	
Explains jokes based on word play (e.g. a joke like: *A Bear Chased Me Up a Tree by Claude Bottom*).	

Case Study – Memory

Joe is 11 years old. He remembers important events and experiences well. Joe frequently forgets his homework, equipment and lesson times despite lots of reminders. Joe finds it difficult to follow instructions in class and to remember new vocabulary. He struggles to remember the alphabet, months of the year or times tables. Joe gets frustrated with himself and says he 'is useless'. Joe plays in all the school sports teams.

Memory Checklist

Name: _____ Date of Birth: _____	
5 TO 7 YEARS	*TICK*
Knows what activity comes next in daily routine.	
Says the days of the week and months of the year in order and gives own address.	
Remembers what he did at the weekend.	
7 TO 9 YEARS	
Follows a three-part instruction in sequence (e.g. put your books in your tray and, if it is raining, put your coat on).	
Gives the letter or month before or after the one given (e.g. the letter before 'h', the month after May).	
Remembers some events and characters from a story.	
9 TO 11 YEARS	
Follows a four-part instruction in sequence (e.g. put your books in your tray, if it is raining put your coat on then line up at the door).	
Remembers timetable facts.	
Remembers details from class discussion or a story (e.g. the dates of events and the names of characters).	
Knows and uses own best strategies for remembering.	

Case Study – Vocabulary and Concepts

Luke is 7 years old and often misunderstands everyday words. He seems to understand new concepts when they are covered but does not apply his learning to other situations or retain these words over time. When talking, he struggles to remember words although he seems to have a clear idea of what he wants to say. Luke finds it difficult to sort objects into categories, e.g. fruit and vegetables. He sometimes confuses words with similar meanings, e.g. camel/giraffe. Luke reads fluently and has no difficulties with number work.

Vocabulary and Concepts Checklist

Name: _____ Date of Birth: _____	
5 TO 7 YEARS	*TICK*
Asks the meaning of new words.	
Learns and remembers everyday vocabulary (e.g. camel).	
Understands basic concepts (e.g. long/short, heavy/light, above/below, now/later).	
7 TO 9 YEARS	
Uses words accurately in the right situation.	
Learns and links together topic vocabulary (e.g. desert animals).	
Gives the different meanings of words which sound the same – homonyms or homophones (e.g. blue/blew, won/one).	
9 TO 11 YEARS	
Organises and makes links in meaning between words.	
Uses specific vocabulary relating to a particular subject area (e.g. habitat).	
Understands everyday expressions (e.g. butterflies in my stomach, as good as gold).	
Includes detail and expresses ideas with precision.	

Case Study – Understanding

Tasneem is 11 years old, a motivated learner and an excellent artist. Tasneem finds schoolwork overwhelming and worries about homework and exams. Tasneem finds it difficult to make sense of information. She frequently 'misses the point' and does not always link new information with past learning. Tasneem relies a lot on her friends to follow activities in class. Tasneem works hard for exams, copying out and reciting information. When it comes to the exam, Tasneem is often unsure which information relates to which question.

Understanding Checklist

Name: _____ Date of Birth: _____	
5 TO 7 YEARS	**TICK**
Follows simple instructions in context (e.g. go and hang your coat up).	
Answers questions about where? who? what? why? how?	
Predicts what might happen next.	
Knows when he or she has understood and asks for help when needed.	
7 TO 9 YEARS	
Uses the facts given to reach a logical conclusion (e.g. looks at what people are wearing to reach a conclusion about the weather).	
Follows the main idea in a lesson or topic.	
Visualises (pictures) information to help understanding.	
Asks questions to clarify and extend own understanding.	
9 TO 11 YEARS	
Looks for meaning beyond the facts given.	
Evaluates main points in an argument to reach a conclusion.	
Uses a range of strategies to solve a problem.	
Applies previous knowledge and experience to new learning.	

Case Study – Communication

Charlie is 8 years old. Charlie has lots of language and starts conversations about his particular interests: vacuum cleaners and ducks. Charlie often talks at length including lots of detail. It is often difficult to move Charlie on to a different topic or to get a concise answer. Charlie enjoys factual books and activities with a definite answer. Charlie gets little enjoyment from fiction and finds creative tasks a challenge. Charlie is an affectionate and sensitive boy. He finds the social side of school difficult. He tries to join in with other children but does not know how. Charlie often gets upset over things that happen in the playground. He finds it difficult to understand and explain what has happened.

Communication Checklist

Name: _____ Date of Birth: _____	
5 TO 7 YEARS	**TICK**
Works as part of a group, taking turns and sharing fairly.	
Talks about a range of topics and responds to 'social' conversation.	
Suggests what a person may say or feel in a given situation.	
Stays still and looks at the person he or she is talking to.	
7 TO 9 YEARS	
Joins in with others, negotiating plans and activities and taking turns in conversation.	
Gives the listener relevant and sufficient information (not too much or too little).	
Gives own opinion and supports with a reason.	
Uses appropriate facial expression, intonation and gesture.	
9 TO 11 YEARS	
Accepts different roles within a group.	
Extends listener's understanding by intonation and expression, elaborating and rephrasing.	
Considers different points of view.	
Uses facial expression, gesture and language to encourage the speaker or show an interest.	

The Ideal Teacher

'*We are all equally different.*'
Alistair Smith and Nicola Call

These are principles of 'best practice' for all those working with children. Incorporate them gradually into your teaching approach.

Some of the suggestions will be 'second nature', while others will take time to become part of the class routine.

The ideal teacher:

- believes that all children are capable of learning
- has high and realistic expectations of each child
- shares clear goals with the child
- knows each child's strengths and weaknesses
- is patient with children who need longer to think and answer
- acknowledges that different children learn in different ways and can change her teaching approach to suit different learning styles
- uses a teaching approach that allows the child to **see, hear** and **do**, as they learn
- helps children to think about how they learn and remember
- acknowledges that children with any learning difficulty will find it harder to concentrate than other children
- allows children with difficulties more frequent breaks from learning
- breaks tasks and learning down into small chunks for the child with any difficulty
- involves others to help the child: buddies, helpers, assistants, canteen staff and family at home.

The Ideal Classroom

The ideal classroom is often very hard to achieve. These are principles of 'best practice' and should be worked towards gradually.

The ideal classroom is:

- **quiet** – a place where noise levels and distractions are kept to a minimum. Allow for quiet discussion between children as this is often an effective way of learning
- **calm** – where everyone in the class knows how to work with respect for others
- **structured** – where everyone knows the rules and routine
- **positive** – with tangible rewards for effort as well as success, stars, stickers, certificates
- **organised** – with different spaces for different activities. Where there is at least one quiet space for individuals or groups to work
- **supportive** – allows for children to sit near 'buddies' to encourage co-operation, learning and peer tutoring
- has an analogue clock with all twelve numbers on its face.

Listening and Attention

'We all process information through our senses.'
O'Connor and McDermott

Listening and attention go together since it is only when a child's 'attention' is gained that he can 'listen'. Children need to be good listeners if they are to learn effectively. It is the acquisition of good listening skills that allows complex learning to take place.

Good listeners look at the speaker as they listen. Good listeners know what to pay attention to and what to ignore.

Poor listeners, on the other hand, may not attend and look at the speaker. They may be easily distracted by noise, or they may be confused and inattentive. For them, the classroom can be a difficult place to learn.

Good listening skills help us to take part in conversation and to make friends. Poor listeners may not fully understand what is being said and not know how to take turns in conversation.

Listening in the classroom

Classrooms can be busy, lively places. Noise is made by children in the classroom talking and moving about. Noise is heard from outside as people move about the school. Children learn to ignore distracting noises so they can concentrate, in the same way as most people are not consciously aware of bird song and traffic noise.

Locating sounds

Locating where a sound is coming from is a listening skill. It could be finding where the teacher is when she calls everyone to attention. It could be the sound of a book falling on the floor. Some children in school will not be good at this. As a consequence, they will take longer to 'tune into' the important things going on in the classroom.

Discriminating sounds

Discriminating between similar sounds is another listening skill. Being instructed to 'play' and mishearing this for 'pray' could have embarrassing consequences.

Listening and memory

Good listening relies on memory and understanding. Children may need to remember what they have heard over a period of time. They also need to understand what they have heard.

Development of listening and attention

Listening and attention develop hand in hand in a child's pre-school years. A twelve month old baby listens to sounds and voices but is easily distracted. However, by the time he goes to school he has learnt a lot about which sounds to pay attention to and which to ignore.

Listening also needs to have a purpose and to be rewarding.

Some children enter school with little idea of how to listen effectively for learning. They may not know how to listen to important information. However, listening skills can be taught and improved upon if they are weak.

Problems in listening and attention may be the result of a weakness in phonological awareness, memory, vocabulary, concepts or understanding. It is important to consider all these areas when helping children with listening and attention.

Listening and emotional factors

Some children may have problems listening because of emotional reasons. If a child's mind is distracted by emotional upset, he may not be able to listen effectively for learning. He might have 'good' and 'bad' days. It is not the purpose of this resource to offer solutions for children whose main difficulties are of an emotional nature.

Help With Listening

Teacher strategies

- **Minimise the noise and distraction in the class.**
  Noise and distractions make it harder for children to focus on what is important.

- **Wait for children to be calm, quiet and in a receptive state before you start to speak.**
  Any distraction can make it hard for them to concentrate on what you have to say.

- **Make sure you have the children's attention before you start to speak.**
  Most children find it helpful to look towards the speaker in order to listen effectively. (Children who are on the autistic spectrum may feel very uncomfortable making eye contact. Therefore they should not be made to look at the teacher.)

- **Tell children why they are listening.**
  Listening needs a purpose that is clear to the child, e.g. 'You need to listen so you know what to do next.'.

- **Tell the pupils how long they need to listen for.**
  This will help them keep listening until you have finished, e.g. 'Keep listening until I've told you about the sound we're learning today.'.

- **Allow periods of silence so children can think.**
  The teacher's voice can be a distraction when children need to think.

- **Allow children to have more frequent breaks from learning.**
  Children with poor listening skills tire more quickly than other children.

- **Ignore minor fidgeting or wriggling.**
  This may help some children to listen better.

- **Help the child to be comfortable and ready for listening.**
  Think about the temperature of the room, hunger and thirst, all of which can distract a child from listening.

- **Allow the child to sit in a way that he is comfortable.**
  If children are uncomfortable they will find it harder to listen. Sitting cross legged on the floor may be comfortable for some but not others.

- **Sit the child amongst other children who are good listeners.**
  This will reduce distractions and act as a model for being a good listener.

- **Teach children what to say if they have not heard you clearly.**
  Poor listeners need to know how to ask politely for a repetition or a louder voice.

- **Teach children what to pay attention to in the playground and at lunch time.**
  These situations are noisier than the class and can be especially difficult for the child to listen and attend.

Help With Listening

Child strategies

- **Look at the teacher when she is talking to you.**
  It makes it easier to listen when you look at the speaker. It also tells the teacher that you are listening.

- **Listen until your teacher has finished talking.**
  This will help you listen and concentrate on all the teacher's ideas.

- **Have only what you need on your desk.**
  Distractions make it hard to listen and concentrate.

- **If you find it hard to keep still when you are listening, agree with the teacher what you can hold in your hands quietly.**
  Just holding something can help you to listen and focus better.

- **Sit next to children who are good listeners.**
  They will be good models for you to copy.

- **Tell the teacher if there are noises or distractions that make it hard to concentrate.**
  Then you will be able to listen better.

- **Sit in a place where you can listen easily.**
  Choose the place with least distractions for you.

Listens to a Story in a Group Situation

Photocopiable sheet 1.1

1. Choose a short story with a small number of characters.

2. Have counters ready in the middle of the table.

3. Give each child the name of a character in the story.

4. Read the story. Whenever the child hears his character's name he takes a counter.

5. The winner is the person with the most counters at the end.

Getting Started and Keeping on Task

Photocopiable sheet 1.2

Some children need a mental 'checklist' so they 'know' when they are ready to start an activity.

1. Ask the child to sit where he will have least distractions.

2. Perhaps, sit him next to a peer who can work independently but who is also willing to help him.

3. Make sure the child is listening by asking him to look at you.

4. Discuss what materials he thinks he will need to do the activity.

5. Make it clear to him how he will know he has finished, e.g. 'You will have finished when you have done all ten sums.'

6. Tell the child how long he has to complete the activity.

7. Give frequent positive feedback so he knows he is keeping on task, e.g. 'You are concentrating well. Keep this up and you will finish all the sums.' 'You have concentrated for three minutes. Well done!'

8. Build up the amount of time poor listeners are expected to listen for.

9. Work out a signal to tell the child they have lost focus. For example, a card with a picture on one side to show sitting and concentrating and daydreaming on the other side. The teacher would quietly turn over the card to daydreaming if the child had lost focus and turn it back when he was 'on task' again.

Focuses on an Activity, Ignoring Noise and Distractions

Photocopiable sheet 1.3

1 'Listening walk' around the school

The first activity is to identify the different sounds in the school or class environment.

Then the aim is to identify the distracting noises and note the sounds to pay attention to.

1. Go for a walk around the class or the school. Listen to and identify the sounds you hear.
2. Locate where the sound is coming from.
3. Decide with the child which sounds are 'loud' and 'quiet'. The child may have a different perception of this to an adult.
4. Decide if the sound should be ignored, e.g. someone walking along the corridor, or paid attention to, e.g. the bell for lunch.
5. Help the child to focus on one sound at a time if there are several going on at once.
6. List or draw pictures for the sounds.

2 Ignoring noises while working on a task

1. Set the child a short activity to do.
2. When he is distracted by a noise, find it on their list or chart.
3. Ask the child to make decisions about how to respond to the noise.
4. If it is a 'distracting noise' ignore it and go back to the task.
5. If it is a sound to listen to, stop working and pay attention to it.
6. Then go back to the task.

Takes Turns and Waits in Conversation

Photocopiable sheet 1.4

[1] Use the 'Good Listening' strategies poster to show what the child can do to be a good listener.

[2] Praise peers who are listening to what others have to say. Make it clear why you are praising them. Say, 'Good listening, Michael, you put up your hand to ask your question.'.

[3] Reward the child for doing any of the 'Good Listening' points. Verbal praise or a sticker might be appropriate.

[4] Tell the child to '**use** their ears and **think** about the words', before asking a question.

[5] Give the child the opportunity to be the leader in an activity. They can then become aware of the contribution of other members of the group.

Cont'd

'Good listening' strategies

 *Look at the person talking.*

 Listen to what they have to say.

 *Think about the words you hear.*

 *Sit still.*

Stay quiet when you are listening.

 Ask questions to show you have been listening.

Listens Carefully during a Class Activity

Photocopiable sheet 1.5

This activity requires more complex listening and attention.

1. Give each child the picture sheet that accompanies the extract.

2. Ask the child to name the pictures.

3. Read the accompanying extract from a story.

4. Ask the child to circle each picture as they hear the words in the story.

From Problems with a Python *by Jeremy Strong*

Adam pressed his nose against the glass tank.

'It doesn't look like a very big snake,' he told his friend.

Gary rolled his eyes.

'That's because she's curled up round herself,' he said. 'I'm telling you, she's over a metre long. Anyhow, she's not meant to be that big.'

'I thought pythons were huge.'

'Not when they're small,' Gary pointed out simply. 'They have to be small first of all. This one is a baby – well, a toddler at any rate.'

Adam tapped the glass, but the snake didn't budge. 'What do you feed it on?'

'She's not an "it" and you won't need to feed her,' answered Gary. 'We're only going away for a week to stay with my Gran.' He looked lovingly at the snake. 'She won't need a meal for days. She ate a whole rat last night.'

'Urrgh! That's revolting,' said Adam.

'What do you expect pythons to eat? Jelly babies? Ice cream?'

Cont'd

From: *Problems with a Python* by Jeremy Strong, published by Barrington Stoke.

Knows what to do to Listen and Focus on an Activity

Photocopiable sheet 1.6

[1] Discuss with the child what distracts them from their learning.
'I get distracted by ...'
'I find it hard to listen when ...'

[2] Find practical solutions to these distractions. For example, the child might need to sit next to someone different.

[3] Ask the child what helps them to focus and listen.
'I would listen better if I could ...'

[4] Find practical ways to help them focus. Provide a cushion if this stops them fidgeting on the chair. A stress ball to squeeze in their pocket can help some children.

[5] Make a small checklist of the agreed positive things the child can do. Keep this on their desk.

Get started and keep on task

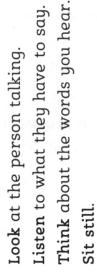

Take turns in class activity

Look at the person talking.
Listen to what they have to say.
Think about the words you hear.
Sit still.
Stay quiet when you are listening.
Ask questions to show you have been listening.

Listening to a story

Listen out for the main person in the story.

Work on a task and ignore noises

Phonological Awareness

'Are we doing cinnomons and ossopites today?'
(synonyms and opposites)

Martin aged 11

Phonological awareness is the ability to split and blend together sounds within words. It is a skill dependent on the development of good listening skills.

Phonological awareness consists of knowing about:

- **Word boundaries** – the way we speak can be split into units of meaning called *words*.
- **Syllables** – words have beats that can be clapped out, e.g. pi – lot (two beats). The number of syllables relates to the number of vowels that can be heard in a word.
- **Rhymes** – words can share the same sounds at the end 'tray, day'. (This is the last vowel and consonant combination.)
- **Alliteration** – when words have the same sound or sounds at the beginning, e.g. 'the blue ball bounced in the box'. Four words beginning with 'b'.
- **Morphology** – word beginnings or endings (prefixes or suffixes) which add meaning to the word.

> **example**
>
> un + well = unwell or 'not well'
> dog + s = dogs, more than one dog.

- **Phonemes** – the smallest individual sounds that a word can be split into: man, m-a-n.

Phonological awareness and reading

Phonological awareness begins to develop in the pre-school years and is a good indicator of early reading success. Children who have developed phonological awareness skills when they start school are ready to learn to read and spell.

Some children, however, have poor phonological skills and are *not* ready to read and spell. They might not have experienced playing around with sounds and rhymes in words during their pre-school years. Other children may have had ear infections that made it harder to learn about sounds. Other children have poor phonological skills because of a *specific learning difficulty*.

Phonological awareness and speech

Children with phonological awareness difficulties may have unclear speech.

Their problems with phonological awareness may be a result of a weakness in listening skills and memory. It is important to consider these areas when helping them.

Help With Phonological Awareness

Teacher strategies

- **Give visual clues to spoken information about phonological awareness.**
  Clapping the number of syllables, showing with counters, or watching the chin drop with each syllable can make more sense than explaining about them.

- **Show how words in text have spaces between them.**
  Some children do not know that we divide what we say into 'words'.

- **Use magnetic letters to show how words can be split in different ways, e.g. syllables, (win-dow), onsets and rimes, (c-at) individual sounds (h-o-p).**
  Some children prefer a tactile or visual approach to their learning.

- **When children have difficulty 'hearing' the difference between two sounds, use plastic or magnetic letters to show the sounds.**
  Showing the visual difference can help the child begin to understand that they must sound different.

- **Show 'words within words'. Point out what may seem obvious to you, e.g. 'up+side down'.**
  This helps with phonological awareness and understanding the words.

- **Teach that by adding beginnings and endings to words the meaning can change.**
  Make this a listening and showing activity. Children may 'hear' the sounds better once they can 'see' the endings, e.g. 'land' + ed = land<u>ed</u>.

- **Show and discuss how similar sounding words are different, e.g. flat – flap, washing – watching.**
  Seeing the contrast can help children to 'hear' the difference.

- **Speak clearly and slowly and let the child see your mouth.**
  Much information is contained in the mouth and lip movements we can see.

- **If a child is having difficulty making the right number of syllables, say the word slowly for the child.**
  Slowing speech down can enable children to 'hear' the information.

Help With Phonological Awareness

Child strategies

- **Look at the person's face when they are talking.**
  The shape of the mouth tells you information about the sounds being made.

- **Listen for words that start with the same sound or sounds.**
  Finding patterns in words can help you to say and remember them.

- **Listen carefully to the ends of words.**
  Ends of words are harder to hear than the beginning of words. The ends of words often convey the exact meaning, e.g. loving, lovely.

- **Listen and look for words that have rhyming patterns at the end.**
  These words can be grouped together which helps in remembering them.

- **Listen to how many syllables words have.**
  When you can say the right number of syllables, words can be easier to hear, spell and read.

- **Be sure to learn the names and sounds of the alphabet.**
  Understanding the alphabet is a key skill needed to read and spell accurately.

Syllables

Photocopiable sheet 2.1

Some children do not hear the 'natural rhythm' of the language and need to be taught it. To 'hear' syllables children need to hear the vowel parts of a word. Visual and tactile clues must be used to support the listening. This could be the written word and wooden or plastic letters.

Hearing one syllable can be more difficult than hearing more than one.

1. Use curriculum vocabulary or everyday words.

2. Draw pictures or write the words on cards.

3. Say the word first for the child to hear.

4. Ask the child to repeat the word so you know if they can say it correctly. If they can't do this, break the word into syllables for them, e.g. 'news – pa – per'.

5. Use wooden letters to show the child how the words are divided into syllables.

6. Clap the beats as you and the child say the word together.

7. Ask the child to say and clap the word on his own.

8. Say and clap the word three times at speed.

9. Say the word in a sentence or phrase with the correct number of syllables.

Cont'd

Variation 1

Syllable flaps

[1] Take a strip of paper.

[2] Fold it in half.

[3] Open the paper and write the word on the bottom half of the paper.

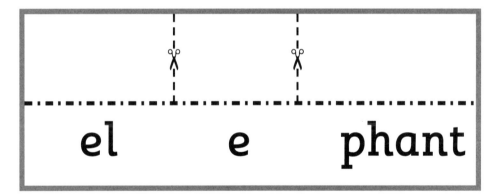

[4] Mark a line on the top half of the strip, where each syllable divides.

[5] Cut along the lines to make flaps.

[6] Open each flap to read if the syllable is correct.

[7] Open them all in turn and say the syllables so that you make a word.

Cont'd

Photocopiable sheet 2.1

Variation 2

Syllable box

1. Divide a shoe box into 6 sections using card.

2. Label the sections 1 – 6 for the number of syllables it represents.

3. Using the everyday and curriculum cards say the words and put them in the section in the shoe box that corresponds to the number of syllables in the word.

Variation 3

Syllable snakes and ladders

1. Use a snakes and ladders board.

2. Put the syllable words in a pile face down.

3. In turn, take a word from the top of the pile and move the same number of spaces as the syllables in the word.

Rhyming words

Photocopiable sheet 2.2

Variation 1

Rhyming names

1. Make up short rhyming sentences using the names of familiar people in the family and class, e.g. *'Mike rode his bike'*, *'Ellie ate some jelly.'*.

Variation 2

Rhyming Bingo

1. Have pairs of rhyming words on blank playing cards, one word per card, e.g. cat, hat, glorious, victorious.

2. Make up blank Bingo boards with nine spaces on each.

3. Place one of the pair of rhyming words on each space on the Bingo board.

4. Shuffle the rest of the cards and place them face down.

5. Take turns to choose a card. If it rhymes with a picture on your board cover it with the card.

6. The first player to get a line of three words shouts 'BINGO!'.

Cont'd

Photocopiable sheet 2.2

Variation 3

Rhyming pairs

[1] Use the rhyming pictures.

[2] Shuffle the cards and place them face down on the table.

[3] Take it in turns to pick up two cards.

[4] If the two cards rhyme, keep them.

[5] The winner is the person with the most pairs.

Alliteration

Photocopiable sheet 2.3

Draw, in sets of three, pictures or words that start with the same initial sound or sounds. Ten sets are a useful number to play a variety of games. Choose words that are easy to show in a picture, e.g. pear, pie, pig.

Support all the activities with wooden or plastic letters that the child can move about.

Variation 1

What's the same?

1. Place all the cards face up on the table.
2. Take it in turns to choose three pictures starting with the same sound. Say the words.
3. Ask the other player to say what sound they all begin with.
4. If the child finds this hard suggest two alternative sounds to choose from. Make the two sounds look and sound very different, /p, l/ **not** /p, b/.

Variation 2

Odd one out

Use the same sets of pictures as the games above.

1. Lay out three pictures, two starting with the same sound and one with a different sound, e.g. pear, hat, pig.
2. Ask the child to say the words and find the odd one (the picture starting with a different sound).

Cont'd

Variation 3

Adjective alliteration

1. Use the sheet of nouns and think of an *adjective* (describing word) to go with the noun that starts with the same letter, e.g. beautiful butterfly, brave butterfly.

butterfly	fish
moon	penguin
hat	tiger
astronaut	sock
duck	slide

Individual Sounds in Words

Photocopiable sheet **2.4**

The train (on page 52) can be used to show sounds represented by a single letter, e.g. h-a-t, or digraph, e.g. sh-i-p. The train can also be adapted to show syllables, e.g. pa-per, or onsets and rimes, e.g. cl-ap.

1. The child should keep a small notebook to record the words you are working on.

2. Choose words the child finds difficult to separate into individual sounds.

3. Use wooden or coloured magnetic letters to support the work.

4. Use the drawing of a train to place each sound in one section of the train.

5. To begin with, provide the same number of sections as the number of sounds in the word. Then the child will just need to focus on the order of the sounds.

6. Discuss 'position' words with the child. This is important since the child may use and understand different words to the teacher. He may use 'at the start' while you use 'at the beginning'. He may not understand the two mean the same thing.

7. It can be helpful to focus on listening to one sound position at a time, e.g. *'Listen for the sound at the end of the word 'stop' and put its letter in the correct carriage on the train.'*.

8. Ask the child to find the sound and place it in the right position on the train.

9. Reverse the roles and ask the child to direct you in this activity, deciding which sound you should listen for.

Cont'd

Hears Suffixes and Prefixes in Speech

Photocopiable sheet 2.5

[1] Choose one prefix (or suffix) at a time, e.g. 'un'. Discuss its meaning, e.g. un = not

[2] Listen for the prefix /un/ in a list of 10 words you say. Tell the child two words will not have the prefix.

[3] Example list:

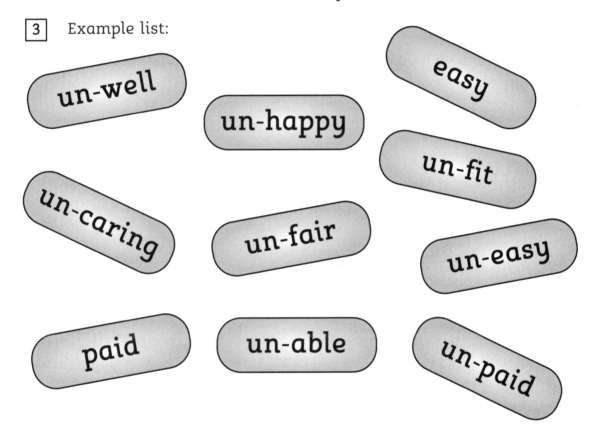

[4] Ask the child to repeat the words after you and decide if it has the prefix.

[5] Use wooden letters to show the word if the child cannot hear the prefix.

[6] Add the words to the child's personal notebook of difficult words.

Hears and Understands Differences Between Words with Similar Sounds

Photocopiable sheet 2.6

- Use similar sounding words that the child confuses.
- Say the words slowly.
- Ask the child to watch your mouth as they listen.
- If they cannot hear the words are different show them how the spelling is different.
- Ask them to have a go at saying the words in the pair, making them different.

Activity 1

Use the words the child confuses and/or the ones below.

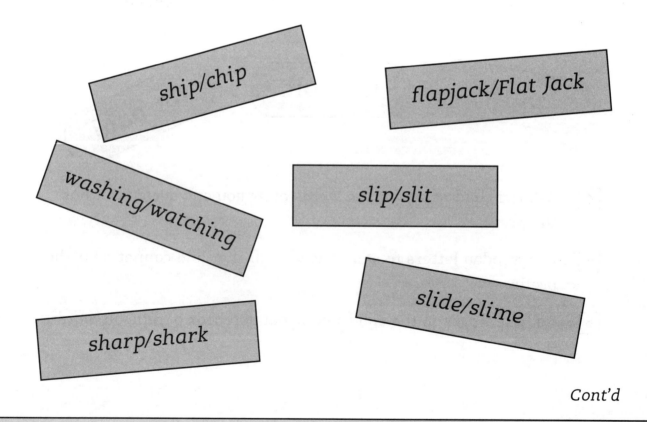

ship/chip

flapjack/Flat Jack

washing/watching

slip/slit

slide/slime

sharp/shark

Cont'd

Photocopiable sheet 2.6

[1] Make two cards for each word. Write the word on one side and draw a picture on the other.

[2] Shuffle the cards.

[3] Place all the cards on the table. Some will have pictures and some will have words.

[4] Take it in turns to find two words that are the same. It does not matter if one is the picture and one is the word. Say the words correctly as you pick up the pair.

[5] If you can't say the words correctly, miss a go.

Variation 1

[1] Shuffle the cards and deal them out.

[2] In turns say a word in your hand.

[3] The other player has to give the correct definition for this word.

[4] If it matches they keep the word.

[5] The person with the most cards is the winner.

Alliteration

Choose a sound.

Find the letter for the sound you have chosen.

Put a ring round the letter.

Write down three words that have this sound at the beginning.

Say the three words.

a b c d e f g h i j k l m n

o p q r s t u v w x y z

1 _____

2 _____

3 _____

Syllables

Use the grid to help you divide words into syllables for spelling.

If you have trouble saying the word correctly ask someone else to say it for you.

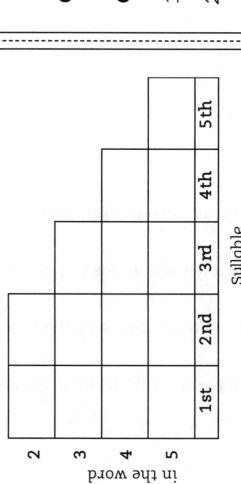

Number of syllables in the word / Syllable

Individual sounds in word

Use the train to help you spell words.

One sound for each part of the train.

Write the letter or letters for each sound in the parts of the train.

Add carriages to the train if you need more.

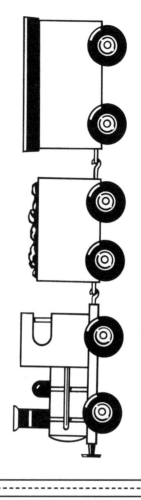

Rhyming words

Choose one word from the list or write your own word in the last box.

Listen for or look out for two other words that rhyme with it.

Write them down in the spaces.

1 peg	1 try	1 lunch
2	2	2
3	3	3
1 play	1 light	1
2	2	2
3	3	3

Listen to sounds at the ends of words

With any difficult spelling words today, have a go at listening for the sound that comes at the end.

Put the letter for the last sound in the carriage with the arrow.

Check with your teacher if you were right.

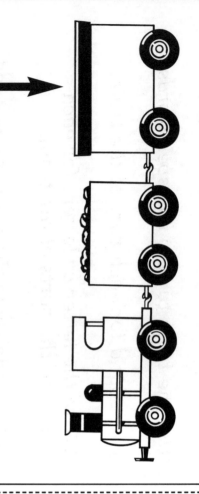

Watching and listening to people speaking

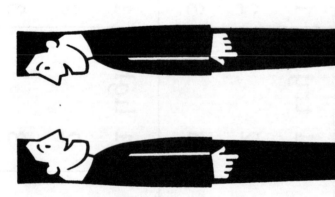

Watch a person's mouth when they speak to you.

Watching can make it easier for you to listen.

Words

These long words have two short words inside them.
Draw a line between the two words.

upse|t   something

birthday   target

overground   laptop

football   sleepover

insight

underground   into

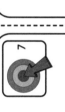

Suffixes

Choose one suffix.

Write or draw the word when you hear it or see it written down.

Listen for three words with this suffix.

–ing
1 ____
2 ____
3 ____

–ed
1 ____
2 ____
3 ____

–s
1 ____
2 ____
3 ____

Memory

'*Memory is primarily a process of making links, connections and associations between new information and existing patterns of knowledge.*'

Robert Fisher

Memory sorts and stores information so we can take in new information and fit it in to what we already know. Our memory acts as a kind of filter for information, deciding what is important to remember and what is not. Some children do not know what is important to *remember* and they can become overwhelmed by the *information* presented to them each day. They can be anxious and frustrated, especially if they are aware of their difficulty.

> **Remembering** – getting back information that has been put into memory.
>
> **Information** – can be spoken and written words, pictures and concepts.

There are three kinds of memory

- **Short-term memory** – used to store a limited amount of information for just a few seconds.

example

Helps us remember which page the teacher has just told us to turn to in our geography book.

- **Working memory** – used to hold one piece of information while working on another piece of the problem. A form of mental juggling.

> **example**
>
> It will enable a child to solve a mental maths problem such as 'add 7 to the sum of 5 and 3'.

- **Long-term memory** – used to store information for much longer periods so it can be retrieved later.

> **example**
>
> Used when a child draws on last term's project of the life cycle of the frog to help them understand this term's project on reptiles.

Each memory has three parts

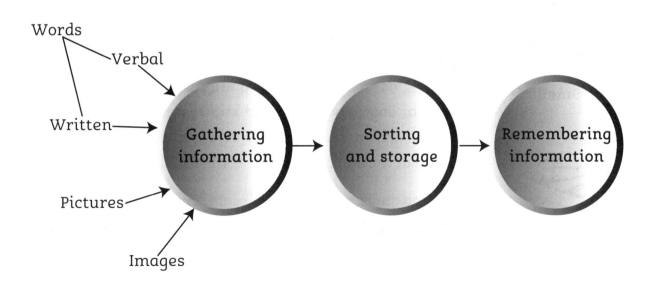

See

Hear

Touch

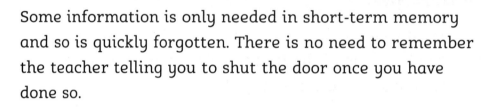
Smell

Taste

Gathering information

We use our five senses as well as words, pictures, experiences and emotions to gather information we want to put into our memories. Since information is presented in many different ways, e.g. words, music, television, food, we need different senses to manage it.

Sorting and storing information

We cannot store all of what we see, hear and experience. Indeed, within 30 minutes of being presented with information, half of it is forgotten.

Some information is only needed in short-term memory and so is quickly forgotten. There is no need to remember the teacher telling you to shut the door once you have done so.

Working memory allows for information to be stored for a little longer while we work out meaning or solve a problem. We need to remember the first lines of a paragraph of text, until we have finished the paragraph and made sense of it all.

We link information we put into long-term memory so that we can manage it all. A child might link the same information in several different ways. He creates a mental 'filing system' where words are stored. So the word 'dog' might be linked to other words, categories and concepts: domestic pets, furry animals, mammals, specific breeds of dogs, dogs the child knows and dogs in story books. Children who are poor at organising information in long-term memory can be overwhelmed by information.

Some learners prefer to use pictures to store information, while others rely more on what they hear. Learners who have inefficient memories can benefit from using other senses to help store information. For example, they might learn how to visualise information if they do not remember sound patterns very well.

Remembering information

Remembering words, facts and concepts is all part of learning.

Not being able to remember information is frustrating for children. They may 'know' a great deal but be unable to tell you *what* they know. Good remembering is about good storage. To remember these words, facts and concepts we need to know where they have been filed in our mental 'filing system'.

Development of memory

Young children remember information in pictures and emotions but as their language develops they remember more and more in spoken words.

When children go to school and learn to read and write, they can also remember information from the written word.

Children develop their memory skills throughout their primary years. In the secondary years, they will need efficient memories to handle increasingly large amounts of information.

Children who have difficulty remembering information may also have poor listening and phonological skills. Difficulties with remembering will also affect understanding. It is important to strengthen all areas of listening and understanding when helping memory.

Help With Memory

Teacher strategies

- **Use pictures to support information, e.g. have a visual timetable.**
  Pictures fix information in memory.

- **Support teaching by writing key words on the board or a sheet of paper for the child to keep.**
  This focuses children on essential information rather than overloading memory.

- **Write homework down as well as saying what it is.**
  This provides a tangible record of the homework to be done. It does not rely on a child's poor memory.

- **Give information in small chunks.**
  This helps with poor short-term memory.

- **Allow children 'thinking' time when they are presented with new information. Tell them this is what it is, 'time to think'.**
  This gives them time to link new information to information in long-term memory.

- **Tell the children what information they will need to remember.**
  This helps them focus on what is essential.

- **Find out the different ways that different children remember.**
  You will be able to adjust your teaching to suit different learning styles and so be a more effective teacher.

- **Make sure children have an understanding of how they memorise information.**
  Children aware of their own strategies are more effective learners. They also like the idea of knowing how the brain works.

- **Repeat and review information you want children to remember.**
  After an hour's teaching, review what has been taught, emphasising the key point. Review again after a week, then after a month. These time scales allow information to be stored in long-term memory. Otherwise within 30 minutes of information being presented half of it will be forgotten.

- **Link new information to what you have already taught. Ask the child how the information links together.**
  A good memory links past and present information. Including the child in making the links makes them active learners.

- **Allow children to write things down as you teach them.**
  Recording information as they go along allows some children to focus on the lesson content.

- **Consider teaching visual learners how to draw pictures, word webs and Mind Maps (Buzan, 1995) for recording information.**
  This organises information into a visual picture which is easier to remember.

- **Tell children the number of parts in an instruction, e.g. 'There are two important things you have to remember ... '.**
  It is easier to remember information in sequence.

- **Repeat information when asked.**
  This gives children confidence that you will help them with their poor memory.

Help With Memory

Child strategies

- **Make pictures in your head of what the teacher is saying.**
  Having pictures in your head is an effective way of remembering information.

- **Find out how you best store information in your memory.**
  Once you know this you can use it all the time.

- **If you remember best by taking notes or drawing pictures, ask the teacher's permission to take notes or draw pictures of the information while she is teaching.**
  Putting down information you might forget allows you to think about what the teacher is teaching.

- **Repeat important information to yourself, either quietly or silently.**
  Repeating information improves your memory of it.

- **Keep a notebook for writing information you need to remember.**
  Writing information down is an effective way of remembering it.

- **Use 'Post-its®' as reminders for things that you need to do. Stick them anywhere you will see them.**
  Post-its® are hard to ignore.

- **When you are taught something new, think of other things you know that link with this information.**
  Making links makes a good memory.

- **Ask the teacher to repeat information.**
  Explain that this helps you remember important information.

Knows What Comes Next in the Daily Routine

Photocopiable sheet 3.1

[1] Use a sheet of card with pictures or photographs to show the main events in the child's routine.

[2] Initially choose only part of the day, for example up to morning playtime.

[3] Draw the main events or take photographs of the child doing the activities, e.g. hanging up their coat, sitting on the floor, registration, learning sounds (literacy hour), snack and playtime.

[4] As each activity starts, ask the child to place the appropriate picture in the right order on the card. Use Blu-tack® or Velcro® so the pictures can come off or be rearranged.

[5] As the child understands the routine, ask him to predict what he thinks will happen next.

[6] Eventually, at the start of the day, ask the child to put all the pictures in order.

[7] Use this chart to show a change in the routine.

[8] Build up to showing the day's routine through pictures that can be placed in any appropriate order for the day.

A quarter to nine	Nine o'clock	Ten past nine	Ten past ten	Half past ten
8:45	**9:00**	**9:10**	**10:10**	**10:30**
Line up	Registration	Literacy Hour	Assembly	Break

Photocopiable sheet 3.2

Remembers the Days of the Week in Order

1. Use the 'Days of the Week' template on the next sheet to draw pictures for each day to illustrate a regular routine. Make it personal to the child.

2. Talk about the week as they do this.

3. Link the events with the names of the days. Make up a story about the week and personalise it for the child, e.g. 'On Monday, Charlie went for his swimming lesson after school. On Tuesday he had PE in the hall and ...'.

4. Use the chart to help the child remember what will happen in the holidays, e.g. Christmas or other religious festivities, summer holiday.

5. Use the chart as a reminder for things in the week, e.g. swimming gear ready on Sunday to take to school on Monday.

Variation 1

Remembers the months of the year in order

1. Use the 'Months of the Year' template to make a personalised chart for the child. Enlarge to A3 if possible. For primary children, it has proved most effective to divide the year up in the way we have indicated.

2. Draw events such as birthdays, holidays, bonfire night and religious festivals.

3. Add the seasons to show how they relate to the months.

4. Make up a story about the events in the year making it personal to the child.

Cont'd

Photocopiable sheet 3.2

		M	T	W	Th	F	S	S	
The week									The weekend

		M	T	W	Th	F	S	S	
The week									The weekend

Cont'd

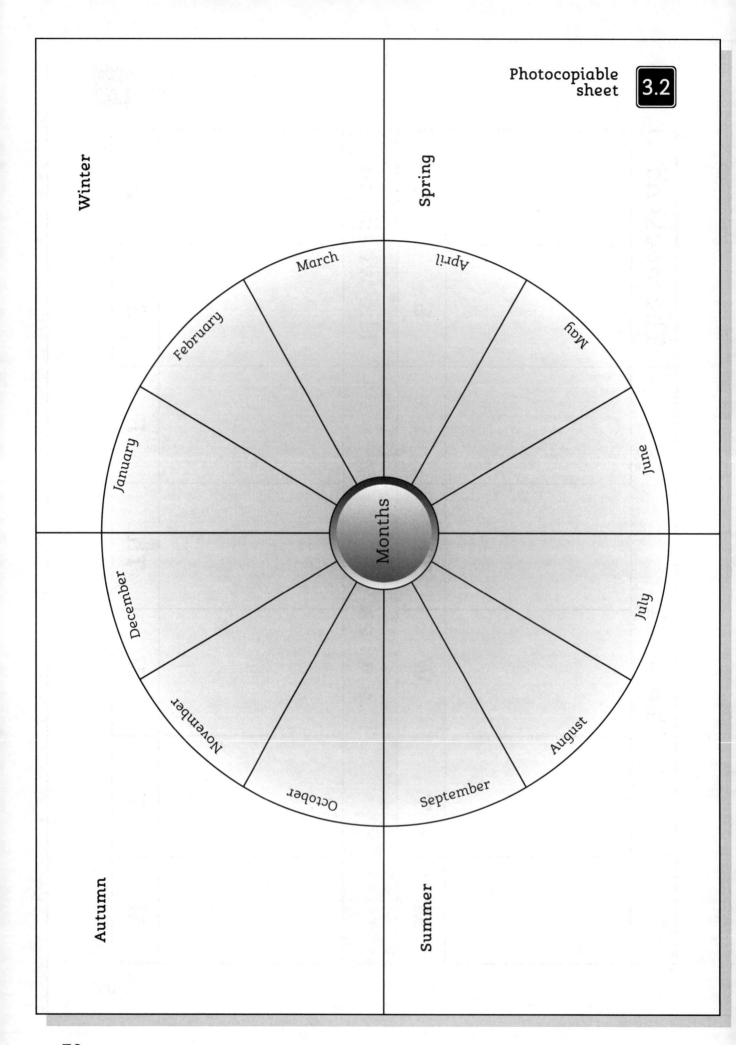

Remembering Events at the Weekend

Photocopiable sheet 3.3

| Seeing | Hearing | Feeling | Smelling | Tasting |

   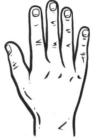

1. Discretely ask the person who brings him on Monday what the child did at the weekend.

2. Use the senses and emotions to help the child remember what they did at the weekend. Ask questions such as: 'What did you see?', 'What did you hear?', 'Can you remember the feel of something nice/horrible?', 'Did anything have a smell that you remember?', 'What did you eat at the weekend?'.

3. Draw pictures to show the answers to the questions.

4. Add words and sentences if appropriate.

5. Put the pictures in the order in which they occurred. Or add more detail to the pictures using the senses questions to jog his memory of events.

6. Ask the child to tell someone else what he did at the weekend, using the pictures and words as reminders.

Follows a Three-part Sequence

Photocopiable sheet 3.4

This will focus the child on remembering a set amount of information. If he has difficulty you will need to support instructions with gestures, words or pictures.

1. Give the child three counters.
2. Give him instructions that have one, two or three parts.
3. Ask the child to put down a counter for each instruction you say.
4. Ask the child to repeat, in his own words, the instructions you gave.
5. Reverse the roles with the child to check if he understands the task.

One-part instruction

- Stand up.
- Write your name.
- Turn to look at the person next to you.

Two-part instructions

- Find your handwriting book and sharpen your pencil.
- Get out all the soft balls and put them next to the teacher's desk.
- When you have finished this sentence, put your book back in your tray.

Three-part instructions

- First wash your hands, second put on a painting apron and third choose a paintbrush.
- Bring me your reading book and if you have finished reading it, choose a book from the reading corner.
- Collect in all the pencils, give out all the maths books and then sit down with your arms folded.

Remembers Details from Class Discussion or Story

Photocopiable sheet 3.5

[1] Discuss different ways to remember information: visualisation, grouping items together, sound of the words, etc.

[2] The child has one minute to look at the sheet of pictures on the next page.

[3] The aim is to remember as many things using a memory strategy the child feels works for them.

[4] On a sheet of paper draw or write the items they remember.

[5] How many did the child remember? What strategy did they use? Could they have used a different strategy that would have helped them remember more?

[6] Some children may need to do this activity again with different pictures in order to practise how they best remember.

[7] In what lesson in school could they use this memory strategy?

[8] Agree with the child in which class discussion or story they will use this strategy.

[9] After the lesson, sit down quietly with the child and ask them to recall information from the lesson. This could be as pictures.

Cont'd

Knows and Uses own Best Strategy for Remembering

Photocopiable sheet 3.6

[1] Choose part of a story or a factual piece. Choose something from the child's reading book or a book supporting the curriculum. Photocopy it for the child.

[2] Read the piece with the child.

[3] Ask him to visualise, write notes, draw pictures, or make a mind map of the information he has read/heard.

[4] Help him to do this, starting with the main idea and then adding the details.

[5] Within an hour of starting the task, review the information by asking the child to explain what he has written down or drawn.

[6] Ask the child *why* he used his chosen method of recording the information.

[7] Within a week, review the information again.

[8] Within a month review the information, asking the child to tell you what he remembers.

Remembering days of the week

Draw a small picture each day of something you have done.

The week					Weekend	
M	T	W	Th	F	S	S

Know what comes next in the daily routine

Ask the teacher what the next two activities in class will be.

In the correct order, draw a picture for each one (or write a word).

Be the first one ready for the next two activities.

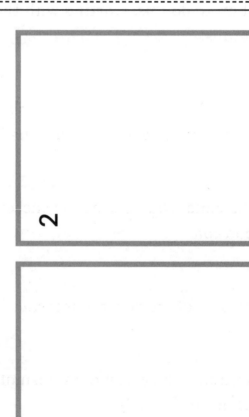

76

5. Remember details from a story or discussion

Who?

Where?

When?

One main event.

A second event.

6. How I remember best

Put a ring round the picture that shows how you remember best.

Use this way of remembering all day today.

3. Remember instructions

Listen and watch. Make pictures in your head.

Write down key words.

4. Remember characters in a story

Draw the main characters of a story the teacher has been telling you.

Do this as soon as she has finished telling the story.

Add as much detail as you can remember.

Vocabulary and Concepts

If I can't picture it, I can't understand it.'
Albert Einstein

'Vocabulary' means words while 'concepts' are broader ideas than single words. So 'dog, help, yellow' is vocabulary while the concept of 'big' could include the words, images and emotions for 'huge, large, enormous, whale, elephant, forest'.

Vocabulary, concepts and links

New vocabulary is taught every day in school. When vocabulary is linked, *concepts* can be formed. Thinking in concepts allows for the organisation of large amounts of information. This is crucial for success at secondary school where new vocabulary and concepts are learnt every day.

Learning new words is not just about understanding. Once children connect words, concepts and ideas they can think in new ways, solve problems, and ask questions about the world around them.

Teaching is language based, so children with poor skills in vocabulary and concepts will be at a disadvantage in school. However, teaching that is supported by visual clues will help these children enormously. Pictures last longer than words and can be easier to remember. They also give information about the meaning of the words and can help in the building of concepts.

Organising information

Some children will need to be taught ways to organise information. Visual clues such as icons, pictures and word webs can make connections between words for the child.

An example of a word web showing how the individual words are connected to the main concept of 'wool' is shown below.

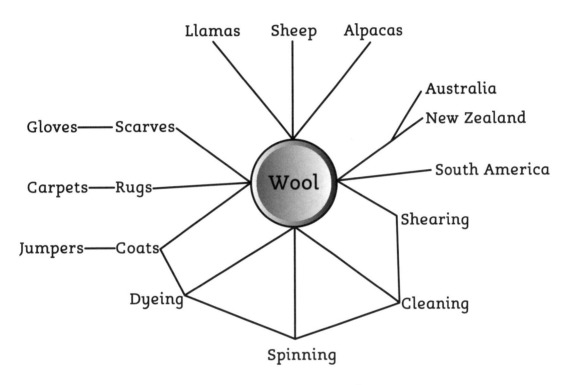

Children who do not easily learn new words and concepts may misunderstand and be misunderstood. They may take language too literally and miss the point in both spoken and written language. For these children, ways to help them understand and remember words and concepts must be a priority in teaching.

When considering how children learn, it is impossible to separate the learning of vocabulary and concepts from listening and attention, phonological awareness and memory. A difficulty in learning vocabulary and concepts may be a result of weaknesses in one of the other areas. It is important to consider all these areas when helping a child to learn new words and concepts.

The language of maths

When children learn maths they bring together many skills to solve problems. Not only do they need to have good memories for the mental maths; they need to know the vocabulary of maths. Consider all the different words that mean 'addition', 'subtraction', 'multiplication' and 'division'.

Some children will make the link between all the addition words and the concept of 'adding'. Other children will need to be told these words mean 'adding numbers together' and may not realise that the concept is the same each time. Others may be good at solving maths problems where only the '+' sign is used but flounder with the words.

The vocabulary of maths is complex and includes many concepts relating to shape, size, position, time, number and quantity.

When helping children who have difficulty with maths, it is necessary to consider weakness in memory, vocabulary and concepts.

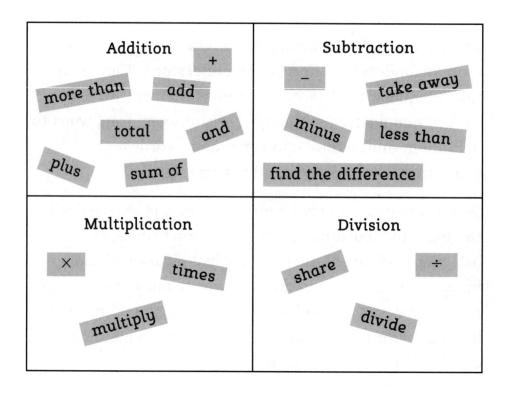

Help With Vocabulary and Concepts

Teacher strategies

- **Use pictures and icons to support the teaching of vocabulary and concepts.**
  This makes word learning more concrete and easier to understand.

- **Teach the difference between 'concept' and 'vocabulary'. The 'concept' is all the words that make up the broad idea, e.g. huge, while 'vocabulary' is the words: big, huge, large, elephant, etc.**
  Children may be unaware they need to know the difference.

- **Choose books which have pictures and diagrams to support the text.**
  Pictures help children to understand information.

- **Teach children how to visualise words they hear. Visualising is making pictures in their heads to remember the words they hear.**
  Visualising information is a powerful way of learning.

- **Show children how to link new words and concepts to things they already know, e.g. 'We've been talking about oxygen. Carbon dioxide is another important gas that is involved in breathing.'**
  Children may not automatically make these links.

- **At the start of the lesson, introduce the main concepts you are going to teach.**
  This will focus children's attention on the new concept being introduced.

- **Define new topic words prior to teaching and supply the child with a list of the main topic vocabulary.**
  This will enable the child to make sense of the topic as a whole. It will enable parents to support the work at home.

- **Review new vocabulary at the end of the lesson in which it was introduced.**
  This links the words in the topic and aids memory of new words.

- **Review recent vocabulary and concepts regularly by asking children to explain what they know.**
  New information, words and ideas will be generated, adding to the links children make to other knowledge.

- **Use familiar words when giving instructions; 'draw' rather than 'illustrate'.**
  Instructions should be clear, particularly when new vocabulary is being taught.

Help With Vocabulary and Concepts

Child strategies

- Make a personal dictionary of words you find difficult to understand. Write the meanings in your own words.
  You will understand and remember better if it is a personal dictionary.

- After a lesson, write down the main vocabulary and concepts and make a word web. For example all the words and information related to 'wool'.
  This will help you link the information and understand it better.

- Practise using a new word in a sentence or in conversation.
  If you are trying out new words you will be learning about them.

- Do something active. Make flash cards with the word on one side and the meaning on the other. Write one sentence on the back using the word and showing you understand the meaning. If you cannot remember the meaning the next time, look at your sentence. Then write another sentence using the word correctly. This will help establish the meaning. Carry on like this until you are sure of the meaning of your new word. Play a game with a friend.
  We learn more when we are involved in the learning.

- Underline in pencil new words when you are reading. Try to work out the meaning from the sentence. Do this by covering the new word with your little finger. Now try to read the sentence and your brain may tell you what the word means. If this doesn't help ask a friend or helper to explain what the word means.
  Being involved in your own learning will mean you understand and remember more of the words and concepts.

- Use colour to group words belonging to the same category or subject. Write them in colour or visualise them in colour.
  This will help your brain organise the information.

Learning New Vocabulary

Photocopiable sheet 4.1

Ensure that vocabulary and concepts are **related to class teaching**.

1. Choose a concept, e.g. 'Life in the Rainforest'. This is **the big picture**.

2. Choose the vocabulary for this concept, e.g. 'snakes, flying foxes, spiders'. This is **the detail**.

3. Create a **word web** called 'Life in the Rainforest'. Show the connections between the words.

4. Make links with vocabulary and concepts the child already knows. Connect these to the word web you have made.

5. Make several interconnecting word webs: rainforest, savannah and tundra.

6. To check the child has understood the concept and vocabulary, make a blank word web. Provide the vocabulary on cards or as pictures. Ask the child to place the vocabulary on the web showing **the big picture** and **the detail**.

7. Ask the child to explain the word web to you or another child.

Variation 1

Odd One Out

1. Use words from the above activity.
2. Choose two of the topic words.
3. Add another word that is not related to the topic and ask the child to find the odd one out.
4. Make the activity harder by choosing four topic words and one odd one.

Learning a New Concept

Photocopiable sheet 4.2

1. Choose a concept, e.g. 'cold'.

2. Use multi-sensory approaches to support the learning. Use real objects, pictures, colours, gesture, investigation, word webs.

3. Find and discuss other words that have a similar meaning to the concept of 'cold', e.g.

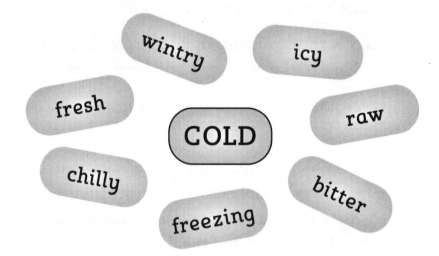

4. Find objects that can be 'cold' e.g.

5. Find words that have the opposite meaning to 'cold'.

6. Think of and discuss other concepts related to 'cold', e.g. Russia in winter, Antarctica, changes in the body when cold.

7. Check learning by asking the child to explain the concept and the linking vocabulary and concepts to another child.

Understanding Homophones

Photocopiable sheet 4.3

[1] Choose **homonyms** or similar sounding words that the child confuses.

[2] Write each word on a blank playing card. Alternatively, draw a picture to illustrate the word.

[3] Shuffle the cards and put them in a pile.

[4] Throw a dice. The number determines what the child has to do.

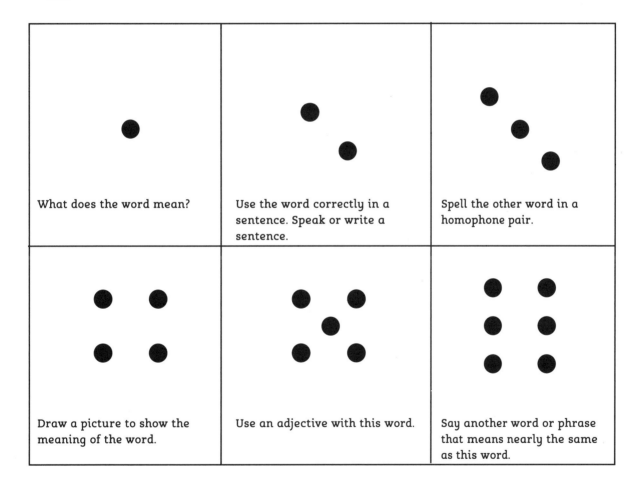

●	●●	●●●
What does the word mean?	Use the word correctly in a sentence. Speak or write a sentence.	Spell the other word in a homophone pair.
●●●●	●●●●●	●●●●●●
Draw a picture to show the meaning of the word.	Use an adjective with this word.	Say another word or phrase that means nearly the same as this word.

[5] When all the cards have been used the winner is the person with the most cards.

Cont'd

Photocopiable sheet 4.3

Starter word list

male/mail	*oar/or*	*wood/would*
there/their	*hour/our*	*hole/whole*
week/weak	*red/read*	*right/write*
won/one	*fir/fur*	*toe/tow*
been/bean	*see/sea*	*fair/fare*

Variation 1

Pairs game

1. Place all the cards face down on the table.
2. Each player takes it in turn to turn over two cards.
3. If they are a matching pair of homophones, keep them.
4. The person with the most pairs is the winner.

Variation 2

Play the game using words that have one spelling but two different meanings, e.g.

May = month   too = as well as

may = doing word   too = more than

Understanding and Using Words Accurately

Photocopiable sheet 4.4

Once the child understands what he should do, reverse the role of teacher and child so the child is asking the questions.

1. Use topic words or familiar words in the child's vocabulary.
2. Write the words on cards or draw pictures for them if appropriate.
3. Put the words face down in a pile.
4. Take it in turns to take a card. The other person asks the questions until they have guessed the word on the card.

Questions

- Tell me five things you know about it.
- What category does it belong to?
- What is it made of?
- What can you do with it?
- Where would you see it?
- What would you use it for?
- What does it feel like?
- What does it look like?
- What sound does it make?

Organising and Making Links Between Words

Photocopiable sheet 4.5

1. Use a word web to show the links between words.
2. Choose a concept that is relevant to the child, e.g. 'food'.
3. Find categories of words that are linked to the main concept, e.g. snacks, meat, fruit, vegetables, etc.
4. Find words that are linked to the categories.
5. Make a skeleton web with some of the words missing. Put the missing words on cards and ask the children to put the words in the right place.
6. Ask the child to explain the web to another child.
7. Revisit the web after two or three days and carry out the activity again seeing what the child has learnt and remembered.

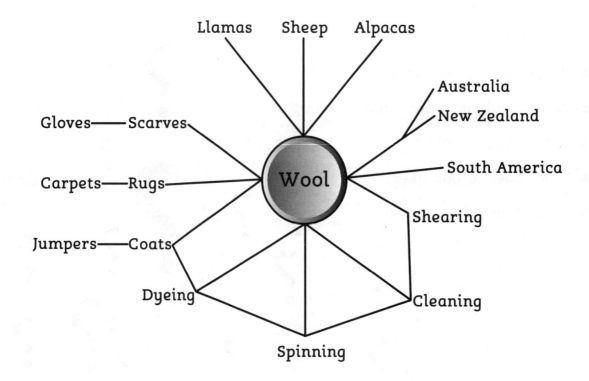

> **Understanding and Using Everyday Expressions and Sayings**

Photocopiable sheet 4.6

1. Explain that when people talk they do not always mean exactly what they say, give an example such as 'You're pulling my leg.'

2. Listen to people in class. Make a list of some of the everyday expressions that are used that mean something different to the words used. For example, 'Some of us got out of the wrong side of the bed this morning', 'I've got a frog in my throat', 'I can feel butterflies in my stomach'.

3. Teach the real meanings of these expressions.

4. Contrast the literal and real meaning of everyday expressions.

5. Draw pictures to show the meanings.

6. Discuss the context in which these expressions might be used, e.g. emphasis or as a joke. 'I'm over the moon' could be interpreted literally if used by Neil Armstrong visiting the moon from a space rocket. It has a different meaning if used by someone whose feet are on the ground but they are very pleased about something.

7. Discuss the situations where these expressions might be appropriate. For example, 'I got caught in a jam this morning', 'I'm over the moon'.

8. Role play with an expression so the children can practise using it and become more comfortable using it.

Learn new words

Choose a new word you have learnt.

Put it in the middle of a word web.

Add other words you know, linking them to the word in the middle.

Explain your finished web to someone else.

Learn a new concept

Make pictures in your head of the new concepts you have learnt today.

Explain these new concepts to someone else.

Use words accurately

Use a new word in conversation today.

Make links between words

Write down three new words you have learnt.

1 _____
2 _____
3 _____

Write down any other words that link by similar meaning, opposite, rhyme or similar sound.

New vocabulary

Make cards for new words.

Write the word on one side and the meaning on the other.

Keep these cards safe so you can check the meaning of the words.

Think about groups of words

*Draw three rings, a red one for **verbs** (doing words), a green one for **nouns** (naming words) and a blue one for **adjectives** (describing words).*

Fill the circles with verbs, nouns and adjectives you hear and read today.

Write the words or draw pictures.

New words in a reading book

Stop and think.

Does it look like any other word you know?

Does it sound like any other word you know?

Re-read the paragraph.

What could the new word mean?

Check with someone that you have the right meaning.

A mind map for new ideas

Draw a mind map of what you have learnt in the lesson.

Use words and pictures and lots of colour.

4 Vocabulary and Concepts   Listening and Understanding in Primary Schools   © J Reilly & S Murray 2004

Understanding

*'She explained what I was to do:
"Like this and like this and like this.
Likethisandlikethisandlikethisandlikethisandlikethis..."
Then she went. I had no idea what she had said.
It had all gone much too fast.'*

Gunilla Gerland

What is understanding?

Children listen to help them understand and think. Understanding is the process by which a listener makes sense of what is heard. It is an important part of thinking.

Understanding involves connecting pieces of information (e.g. facts, dates, names, words and details) together as a whole. It enables children to get the main idea, to draw conclusions and inferences, to make predictions, to extend and evaluate their own thinking.

Understanding and learning

At school, children are faced with ever increasing amounts of information which they must understand in order to make progress with their learning. Since understanding is cumulative, children need to use their existing understanding and knowledge to help them make sense of new ideas and information. Often they must take in and understand information at great speed so they do not miss whatever comes next.

As they get older, information becomes more complex and presented in language which is more difficult to understand. As children encounter different subjects, they have to use increasing amounts of language to understand and think in different ways.

Difficulties with understanding

Most children know when they have understood something. When children have difficulties with understanding they are at risk of giving in or accepting confusion as the norm. These children need to experience what it is to understand. They should be given insight into what understanding involves and strategies to use when they do not understand enough.

Some children have difficulties with understanding because their listening and attention skills are weak. Other children may not be able to remember what is said or understand the vocabulary and concepts being used. It is important to consider all these areas when helping a child to understand better.

Help With Understanding

Teacher strategies

- **Speak slowly.**
  A child needs time to take in and understand new ideas.

- **Allow time for the child to understand and answer.**
  Some children are slow to process information and need time to think about what you have said.

- **Ask the child to repeat in his own words what you have been saying.**
  This acts as a check between teacher and child and tells you how much the child has understood.

- **Use simple sentences that follow the order in which activities are to be carried out. Use words like 'first', 'next', 'last'. Check first that the child understands the words 'first', 'next', 'last'.**
  e.g. First, drink your milk and then go out to play.
  The child will be able to follow a sequence better.

- **Use clear, unambiguous language which is related to the here and now.**
  e.g. 'Try this' rather than 'Take a shot at this'.
  The real meaning of everyday expressions, jokes, puns and colloquial language is not always clear.

- **Give choices when asking questions.**
  e.g. 'Did you go with Amy or Sue?' rather than 'Who did you go with?'
  This will make it easier for the child to give an appropriate answer.

- **Arrange with the child before the lesson that you will ask them a particular question in class. Practise the question and answer beforehand.**
  This is an excellent way of raising self-esteem in front of other children.

- **Teach the child to visualise (picture in his head what he is being asked to do). Turn spoken material into something visual (e.g. models, pictures, written words). Use gesture, facial expression and intonation to make the meaning clear.**
  All these add meaning to what you say.

- **Teach through practical experience and 'doing'.**
  The more senses (seeing, hearing, touching/doing, smelling and tasting) you involve, the more powerful the learning experience is.

- **At the start of the lesson give a clear overview of what is going to be covered. Write or draw this on the board for reference. Explain how long you will spend on each part of the lesson. Recap the main points at the end.**
  For example, *'There are three points that you really should remember.'*
  This focuses attention on the important points and pulls the information together as a whole.

- **Make sure that the current piece of information is understood well before moving on.**
  For example, *'Tell me what you've learnt'* or *'Tell another child what you've learnt'*.
  This makes understanding cumulative.

- **Agree ways in which children can signal when they need help.** Teach the child to use a prearranged code or signal so that he does not have to draw attention to himself.
  Children can take responsibility for their own understanding and maintain self-esteem.

- **Provide opportunities for the child to ask their own questions.**
  Asking questions requires thinking about and understanding the information.

- **Ask fewer more thoughtful questions.**
  For example, *'What do you know already?'*, *'How do you know?'*, *'What if...?'*, *'What might happen next?'*, *'Where is another example?'*.
  Open-ended questions will help the child understand, think and learn.

Help With Understanding

Child strategies

- **Look at the person speaking and think about the words.**
  This will help you listen better.

- **Put your hand up or signal if you do not understand.**
  A friend or teacher can then help. Tell them to explain in a different way so you can understand.

- **Ask your teacher to say it again – some or all of it.**
  You may find it helpful to hear the information again.

- **Ask your teacher to show you what they mean.**
  A demonstration or picture makes it easier to understand.

- **Ask what new words mean.**
  You need to know the meaning of words in order to understand the lesson.

- **Be prepared to say in your own words what the teacher has told you.**
  This is a good way for you and the teacher to check that you have understood.

- **Have another go.**
  People do not usually understand everything the first time round.

Knowing When You Have Understood

Photocopiable sheet 5.1

The traffic light system gives the child a strategy to check he has understood. It links listening and understanding with planning an appropriate answer.

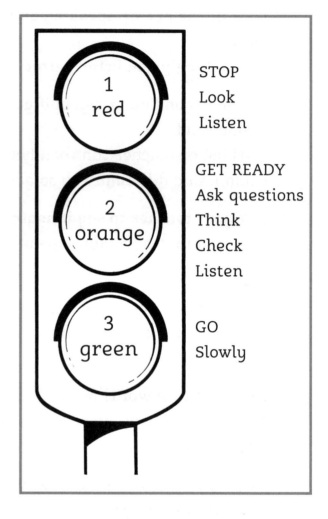

1. **Listening (red)** Tune the child into listening by asking him to 'go into red'. Remind him to stop and listen to all the information.

2. **Checking (orange)** Orange reminds the child to check that he has understood. If he is confused, he can ask questions, find out more information or give himself more time to think.

3. **Go (green)** Once the child 'goes on to green' he should be able to continue independently. If he has forgotten something or needs more information then he should be reminded to 'check at the orange light'.

4. Hang a large set of traffic lights on the wall for all to see. Smaller versions can be given to individual children if required.

5. Use the system regularly across different activities so that the system becomes familiar and part of the class routine. Expect the child to remember the system so he uses it naturally without actual reminders of the 'red', 'orange' and 'green' lights.

Understanding and Using Questions

Photocopiable sheet 5.2

[1] Teach which question goes with which kind of answer. Refer to the 'questions poster' on page 103 when asking the child a question.

[2] Use gestures, colour or written words to distinguish between different question words.

Stick the question words on different coloured pens. Highlight the question word and the answer in the same colour on reading comprehension activities.

[3] Using pictures or topic work, give the child an answer and ask them to make up a matching question.

For example, *the answer 'eight' could match to the questions 'How many legs does the spider have?' or 'How many sides does an octagon have?'*

[4] Swap roles so the child is asking questions to find out information.

[5] Ask the child to help you ask other members of the class questions about the story they are reading or listening to. Have the 'questions poster' on the wall for all to see.

Cont'd

Photocopiable sheet 5.2

Variation 1

[1] Decide on someone to interview. For example, a visitor or an 'expert'.

[2] The child can think up, share, group and choose the best questions.

Variation 2

[1] Teach the child to ask questions before an activity begins. For example, 'What will I need to do in this activity?', 'Who will help me?', 'What do I need to find out?'.

Variation 3

[1] Have a questions box.

[2] Teach the child to put interesting or puzzling questions in the box. At the end of the week, choose a question to discuss in class.

Cont'd

Questions Poster

Photocopiable sheet 5.2

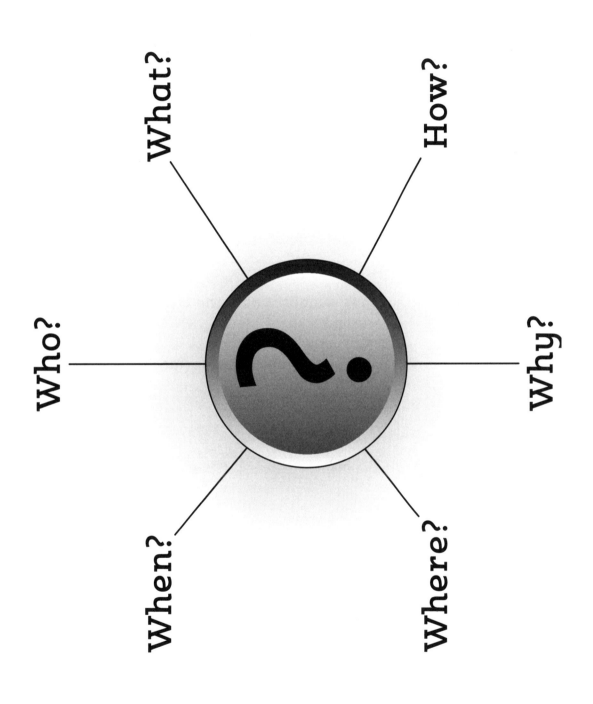

Getting the Main Idea

Photocopiable sheet 5.3

Teach the difference between 'main idea' and 'details'. The main idea is made up of details. The details have to be put together in the right way. Ask the child to give the main idea from a picture containing details.

For example, a picture containing the details: cottage, bears, porridge, adds up to the main idea 'Goldilocks and the Three Bears'.

Variation 1

1. Using a picture, ask the child to talk about some of the details.

2. Then ask for a title, or a few words, which summarises the main idea.

3. Provide two to three suggestions if the child has difficulties with this.

4. Ask the child to select the most appropriate title from those suggested.

Variation 2

1. Read the child a short story.

2. Ask him to suggest or select a title from the two to three you provide.

3. Teach him to include the details which add up to the main idea.

   For example, *'A good title for this story is "Red Beard's Lucky Escape" because there's a pirate called Red Beard. His ship sinks. He rescues all the treasure and swims to an island.'*

Cont'd

Variation 3

1. Choose a book that is easily within the child's reading ability.

2. Ask the child to read a paragraph at a time.

3. Find the word or words which best describe what the paragraph is about. If this is hard, go over the paragraph highlighting the key words (those that carry the most meaning).

4. Discuss how these words add up to the main idea.

5. The child can progress to giving the main idea for a page or chapter.

6. When working on whole chapters discuss how the chapter title may have been chosen. Ask the child to give another title which also summarises the main idea.

Knowing How to Visualise

Photocopiable sheet 5.4

1. Introduce the idea of visualisation.
   'Do you sometimes see pictures in your head? When you visualise it is like having a video in your head. Your brain can see different kinds of pictures. Sometimes these pictures are of things which have already happened to us. Sometimes we use pictures to think about what's going to happen. Sometimes we use our imaginations and make pictures that couldn't possibly be real.'

2. Teach the child to visualise something or someone familiar.
   For example, *his bedroom, pet, friend.*

3. Ask the child to describe the picture.
   'Imagine your bedroom. Imagine where you are standing in your bedroom. From where you are standing, what do you see? What posters do you picture on the wall? What colours do you see?'

4. Get the child to close his eyes to cut out visual distractions. Alternatively, ask the child to move his eyes upwards, keeping his head still. This can help visualisation.

5. Teach the child to include information from different senses.
   For example, *colour, size, shape, sound, smell, movement, feelings.*

   This will ensure that the child relates details together as a whole in his image.

Variation 1

1. Teach the child how to visualise instructions.

2. Show him how to draw simple pictures which include the key words (those that carry the most meaning).

3. Teach the child to relate the words together in a single picture.

4. Then, ask the child to make the pictures in his head rather than drawing them on paper.
   For example, *'Watch a video of yourself carrying out the instruction as you listen to the words.'*

Cont'd

Photocopiable sheet 5.4

Variation 2

1. Read the following passage or a similar paragraph from a story book.

2. Teach the child to visualise or use 'pictures in the head' when listening or reading.

From Mad Iris *by Jeremy Strong*

The ostrich stopped short, just one stride away from where the two children stood rooted to the spot. It fluttered its very long eyelashes and studied them carefully.

What strange birds they were! They had feathers but they couldn't fly. Their knees were big and knobbly. They had the most odd-looking faces.

The ostrich stretched her neck forward and gently touched Ross's nose with her beak. He twitched.

'Hello,' Katie said quietly. 'I like you.'

'Don't be stupid!' muttered Ross. 'You can't *like* an ostrich.'

---

3. Ask the child to mentally make a video recording of the story.

4. Ask questions which help him add detail to the pictures.

   For example:

   - 'What colour did you picture the ostrich's feathers?'
   - 'How many children did you picture?' 'How old were they?'
   - 'What size was the ostrich?'
   - 'Where did you picture the children meeting the ostrich?'
   - 'Was anything moving in your picture?'
   - 'Did your picture have any sounds or talking?'
   - 'Fast forward your video. What did you picture happening next?'

Looking for Meaning Beyond the Facts Given (Inference)

Photocopiable sheet 5.5

1. Use pictures or read the child a short story or part of a story. It may be easier to start with a picture.

From: *The Genie* by Mary Hooper, published by Barrington Stoke

Cont'd

2 Discuss the difference between 'on the lines' questions (which can be answered from the actual information given) and 'between the lines' questions (which involve looking for hidden or inferred meaning).

For example:

On the lines
- What kinds of animals are in the field?

Between the lines
- What time of year is it?
- Is it a weekday or the weekend?
- What might be in the girls' bags?
- Do the girls live in the city or a village?
- Which of the girls has the tidiest bedroom?

3 Emphasise the difference between a guess and an inference. A *guess* is based on imagination, whereas an *inference* is based on careful consideration of the information available and knowledge gained from previous experience.

For example, *there is information to support the existence of a school nearby but not a cinema.*

4 Help the child to decide what type of information is relevant to a given question.

For example, *the presence of leaves on the trees is relevant to the question about the time of year but not relevant when deciding whether it is a weekday or weekend.*

Applying Previous Learning to New Information

Photocopiable sheet 5.6

[1] Before presenting new information, ask the child to recall anything he already knows about the topic.

[2] Draw a 'map' of what the child already knows. Start with the main idea or topic in the centre.

For example, *railway*.

[3] On each thick branch write or draw one important idea that connects with the main topic. Use separate branches for different ideas. If writing, print the word on the branch.

For example, *(railway) station, ticket, track, train.*

[4] On the thin branches write or draw ideas which come to mind in relation to the words or pictures on the thick branches.

For example, *(station) platform, waiting room, guard.*

[5] Use a different colour for each branch to make a visual contrast between different ideas.

[6] Add new information to the relevant part of the map. This will make links in meaning clear.

Cont'd

[1] Colour the four thick branches coming out of the picture.

[2] Use a different colour for each branch.

[3] On the thick branches write or draw important ideas to do with railways.

[4] Write or draw one word on each branch.

[5] On the thinner branches write or draw ideas to do with the words or pictures on the thick branches.

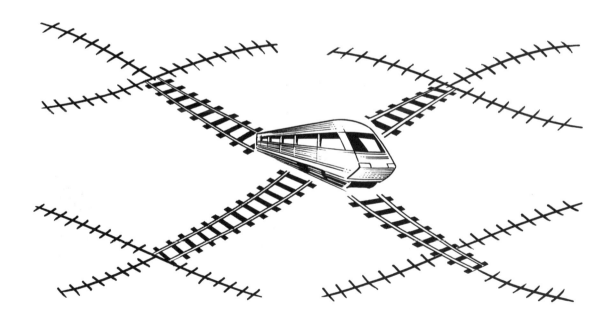

3. Knowing when you have understood

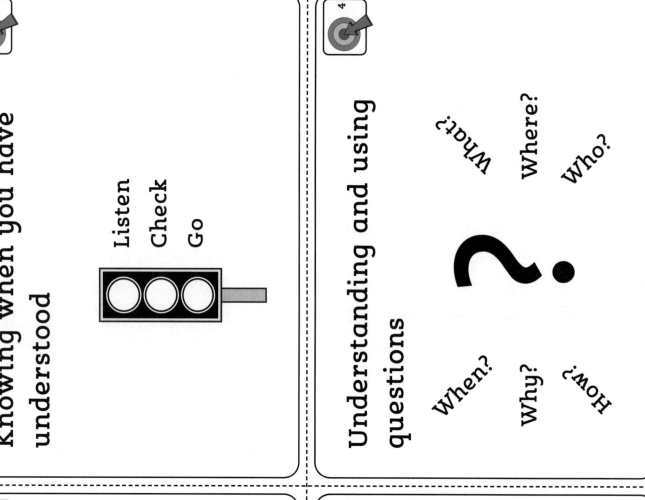

4. Understanding and using questions

1. Help with understanding

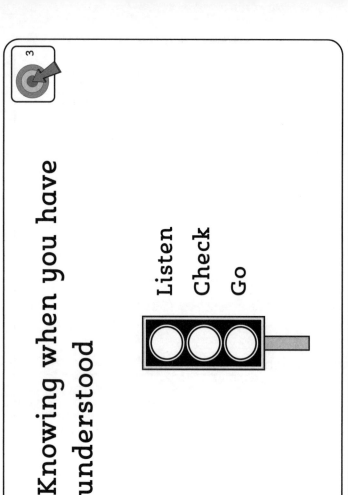

Ask for help.

2. Help with understanding

Look   Listen   Think

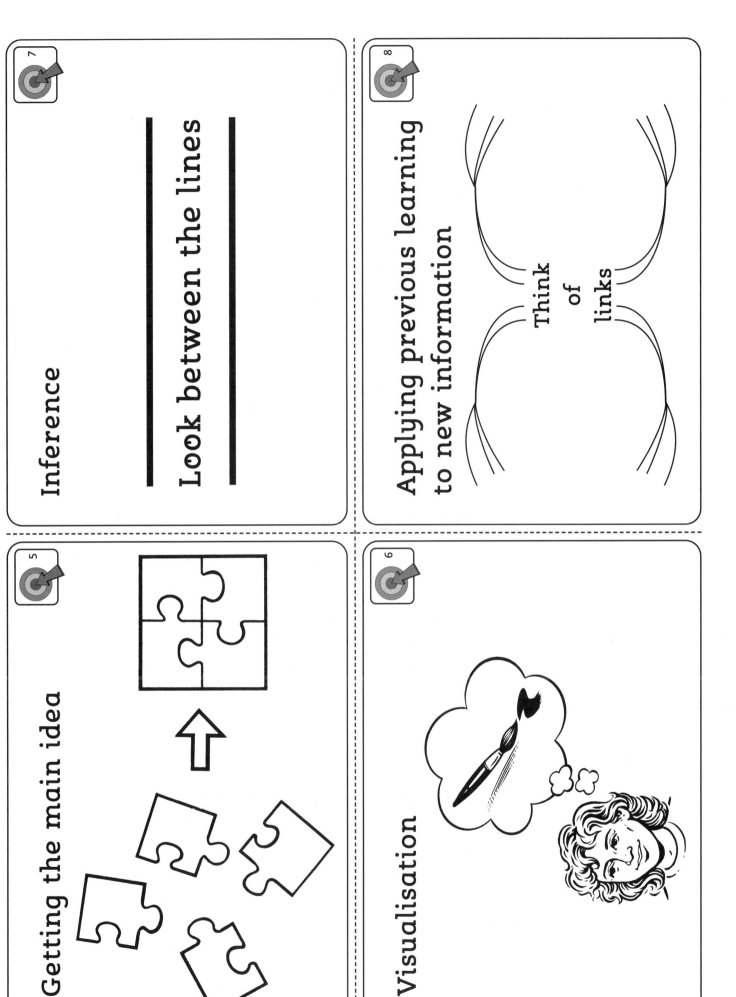

Communication

'I couldn't take part in their games. Three or four children were enough for it to become a confusion of arms and legs, voices and laughter. They frightened me and wore me out. It was like being in a room full of rubber balls in constant motion.'

Gunilla Gerland

Successful communication involves more than language ability. Good communication skills are needed to make friends, share ideas and learn in a group.

Understanding other people

The more sensitive a child is to the feelings of others, the easier he will make friends. Making and keeping friends is vital in developing a child's confidence and self-esteem. The more able a child is to recognise the needs and points of view of others, the more able he will be to make sense of their behaviour and to know when to help, share or back off.

Different uses of language

Language is used in a multitude of ways – asking questions, making requests, expressing thanks, giving compliments or insults, commenting, giving instructions, sharing news, telling stories or jokes, negotiating, explaining feelings, solving problems, promising and so on.

To communicate successfully a child has to achieve shared understanding with another person. If the child is speaking, he has to consider the listener's point of view and be aware of what the listener might already know. This knowledge and understanding will help the child to gauge the right amount to say – not too much and not too little. He needs to check that the other person has understood. When the child is listening, he has to work out what the other person means. This involves knowing when he has not understood and asking the other person to repeat or clarify what they have said.

Talking and learning in a group

Using language in a group is even more complicated. A child has to juggle the needs and points of view of several people. Talking in a group involves sharing turns, showing an interest in what others have to say and giving encouragement.

Learning in a group involves collaborating with others and dealing with problems in a way that respects everyone's needs and feelings. A child needs all these skills as well as being able to listen to and understand the conversation.

Communication is more than just words

Communication is not just about what we say. It is about how we say it and what we do. How we say things includes:

- judging your audience and knowing when to use formal or informal language
- being polite

- using humour at the right time
- using a tone of voice that matches what you want to say
- adjusting language to fit in with the peer group.

What we do when we communicate includes:

- eye contact, facial expression and gesture
- standing at an appropriate distance
- knowing when physical contact is appropriate
- understanding that physical appearance matters.

For most children all these communication skills develop intuitively. Language and communication usually develop side by side and allow the child to learn and make friends effortlessly.

For other children, the social world of school can be confusing. These children do not develop communication skills easily. The unwritten 'rules' for making friends, joining in conversation, being part of a group and understanding other people's behaviour need explanation. The skills underlying successful communication have to be taught so that learning through communication can take place.

Communication is a complex set of skills that may be affected by weaknesses in language. For example, a child with difficulties in understanding will find it hard to take part in a group discussion. When working on communication it is important to strengthen all aspects of listening and understanding. As communication is essential to all aspects of school life, strategies and activities to help with communication should be an integral part of the child's day.

Help With Communication

Teacher strategies

- Establish a set of class rules that are needed for the class to work successfully together. Keep the rules short and simple. Enlist the children's help and agreement.
  For example, *Respect and care for yourself.*
  Respect and care for other people.
  Respect and care for our school.
  The class rules will help everyone work together successfully. It may be necessary to explain the concept of respect.

- **Have a daily circle time.**
  So that the child will be part of a group.

- **Help the child make one or two friends. Set up a buddy system.**
  Then the child will have the support of other children.

- **Provide opportunities for the child to spend time alone if he prefers to do so.**
  This will provide time for relaxation away from the complexities and stresses of a large group. If he has language processing difficulties he will be more tired and benefit from a rest.

- **Use the child's strengths and interests to help him make a meaningful contribution to group activities.**
  This will build self-esteem.

- **Refer to feelings as part of everyday situations.**
  For example, 'You made Michael feel really proud when you said nice things about his painting.'.
  This will teach the child the experience and meaning of feelings.

- **When 'difficult' situations arise, listen to and consider the child's point of view.**
  This will help you understand the child's feelings and the reasons for his behaviour.

- **Talk to the child after the 'difficult' situation.**
  As a result the child will be calmer and more able to consider suggestions and alternatives.

- **Ask the child to talk about, write about or draw the 'difficult' situation.**
  This will help him think of solutions to use in the future.

- **Be patient. Do not assume a child will make connections between one situation and another.**
  Each situation may need to be addressed individually.

- **Make sense of 'inconsistencies' in what a child may say or do.**
  Slight changes, for example, to group size, group composition, teacher, position within the group, activity or language may make the situation easier or more difficult.

Help With Communication

Child strategies

Know how to fit in

- **Watch people's faces and what they do.**
  This will help you notice their feelings.

- **Listen to what other people say.**
  This will help you notice their points of view.

- **Try to picture what it would be like to feel and think the same.**

- **Make new friends slowly.**
  People will be happier if you wait until you know them really well before you act in the same way as you do with your old friends.

- **Make new friends carefully.**
  It is easier to make friends with people who like the same things as you.

- **Be careful how you say things.**
  Say *'Would you like to play a game with me?'* not *'I like you. Let's be best friends.'*
  This is the correct thing to do and is polite.

- **Keep friends happy by thinking about how they feel and what they would like to do.**
  Friends will like it if you say and do things to make them feel good.

- **When you argue, keep calm and think about what to do.**
  Say *'We're friends. It's okay to think differently about some things. Let's forget about this'*, rather than shout or fight.
  This is a better way of dealing with feelings.

- **Watch and listen to other people. If you have upset someone say 'sorry' and ask what you can do to make him or her feel better.**
  It is important to do something about mistakes.

- **Tell people how you feel.**
  They need to know.

- **Think about who you are talking to and choose the right words.**
  You need to talk differently to different people.

- **Talk about things which are connected to what is going on at the moment or things which other people like to talk about.**
  People will be more interested.

- **Give other people time to talk, and listen to what they have to say.**
  This will stop them getting bored and angry and make them feel valued.

- **Always be yourself.**
  People will like you more.

Sticking to or Changing the Topic of Conversation

Photocopiable sheet 6.1

Use these strategies every time you talk with the child.

1. Make the main topic of conversation clear. Signal changes in the topic.

   For example, *'We've finished talking about the heart, now we are talking about the lungs.'*

2. Keep the child on topic. Write or have a picture of the current topic on display.

   For example, *'That's interesting. You can tell me about that at the end of the lesson. Right now we're talking about … '.*

3. If the child returns to the same topic repeatedly, describe your feelings and guide the child towards alternatives.

   For example, *'I'm bored talking about vacuum cleaners. Tell me about your weekend. That will make me happy.'*

4. Provide the child with some opportunities to talk about his interests.

   For example, *'I can't talk about hovercrafts right now. I'll talk to you for five minutes at break time.'*

Cont'd

Photocopiable sheet 6.1

Variation 1

1. Practise sticking to the topic. Choose any topic of conversation.

2. Decide on the number of turns at talking.

3. Use a beanbag to share turns. The person holding the beanbag speaks and then hands it to the next person.

4. Make sure all turns at talking relate to the chosen topic.

Variation 2

1. Practise changing topic. Have a collection of objects in a 'topic box'. There should be two of each object.

2. Take turns to choose an object or 'topic'. The other person 'agrees' to talk about the same topic by finding the matching object. This emphasises that both people in conversation talk about the same thing.

3. Talk about the topic for two minutes remembering to take turns. You could use an egg timer to show the time passing.

Understanding and Controlling Feelings

Photocopiable sheet 6.2

Use these strategies throughout the day.

- Talk about people's feelings and points of view.

  For example, *'You feel angry right now. You think it is Sam's fault. Sam feels confused. He was trying to help.'*

- Keep your voice, your face and your words the same so the message is clear.

  For example, *If you are cross, look cross, say cross words and sound cross.*

- Give the child opportunities to do something else to calm down. This should be the child's choice.

  For example, *Sit in a quiet corner, listen to some music, go outside for a walk.*

Variation 1

1. To help the child develop his awareness of and vocabulary for feelings, use 'how do you feel today?' on page 127.

2. Ask the child to say how he is feeling in different situations at different times of the day.

3. If the child finds this difficult, point to and describe the feeling which is relevant to the situation.

   For example, *'This maths problem is complicated. You probably feel confused about what to do next. Let me explain.'*

4. Make sure the child understands that all his feelings are accepted.

Cont'd

Photocopiable sheet 6.2

Variation 2

1. To help the child control his feelings use the 'How happy are you?' or 'How angry are you?' barometers on pages 126 and 127.

2. Show the child how to use the 'How happy are you?' barometer by referring to it throughout the day.

    'I think you are on 4 and very excited. It is making it difficult for you to listen and concentrate. Try and get back to 3. Tell me when you are ready.'

3. Ask the child to move down the barometer one space at a time. This will make sure that he gains good control over his feelings. He will become more aware of and able to manage escalating or strong feelings.

4. Ask the child to describe what he did to control his feelings. This will make him more able to do the same thing another time.

5. If he finds controlling his feelings difficult, teach the child strategies.

    For example:

    - *'I noticed you were breathing more slowly.'*
    - *'Your face looks calm now. You made the muscles relax.'*
    - *'I saw that you rested your head on the table and closed your eyes.'*
    - *'It was helpful for you to sit on the cushions for three minutes.'*

Cont'd

Photocopiable sheet 6.2

How happy do you feel today?

Cont'd

How Happy are You?

Photocopiable sheet 6.2

hysterical 5

excited 4

happy 3

satisfied 2

calm 1

Cont'd

How Angry are You?

Photocopiable sheet 6.2

furious	5
angry	4
annoyed	3
thoughtful	2
calm	1

Using Appropriate Facial Expression and Gesture

Photocopiable sheet 6.3

Use these strategies throughout the day.

- Use natural facial expression and gesture yourself.

- Describe how you can guess how a person is feeling from what you see (their emotions, **and** their physical state).

  For example, 'Your face is red and you're sweating. You feel hot.', 'Your eyes are twinkling and you're smiling. You're happy.'

Variation 1

1. Teach the meaning of facial expression and gestures through miming activities.

2. Mime the action shown in the pictures on page 129.

3. Ask the child to guess the action.

4. Give the child a turn to mime the meaning of a picture.

5. Progress to miming facial expressions (use the pictures from the 'How do you feel today?' poster on page 127 or the meanings of words (write words on pieces of card).

Variation 2

1. If the child uses too much gesture, get him to hold something or use his pockets to keep 'still hands'.

Cont'd

Helping the Listener Understand

Photocopiable sheet 6.4

The game described here uses the different Grans who appear in the story 'The Crazy Collector' by Diana Hendry, published by Barrington Stoke.

1. Sit either side of a barrier. The child is the speaker. You should take the role of listener.

2. You will both need a copy of the picture on page 134 and some coloured pens.

3. The child instructs you how to colour the picture in. The child should colour his picture in at the same time.

   For example, *'Find the Gran with the short curly hair and glasses. Colour her hair brown and her glasses green.'*

4. The child's target is to give you instructions which include all the information you require.

5. Your role is to provide feedback to the child about the accuracy of his instructions. Either respond appropriately or indicate when you are confused and the type of information you need.

   For example, *'You told me to find the Gran with glasses. Four of the Grans have glasses. I'm not sure which Gran you mean. Tell me more about what she looks like.'*

Cont'd

[6] When the child gives an accurate instruction, describe why it was easy to understand.

For example, *'That instruction was great! You gave me lots of detail about what the Gran looked like and which colours to use.'*

[7] At the end of the activity compare the pictures. The child will receive instant feedback about how well he helped you to understand.

Variation 1

[1] The same activity can be repeated with identical sets of objects or shapes.

[2] The child should arrange his set of objects into a pattern and then instruct you to make the same pattern.

Variation 2

[1] Swap roles. Teach the child to identify when your instruction was not accurate and to ask for the missing information.

Variation 3

[1] Remove the barrier so the child can watch you carry out his instructions.

[2] Follow the child's instructions exactly, even if he misses out important information.

[3] The child's target is to check that you are following the instruction and to realise when and how to change his instruction to make it easier to understand.

Cont'd

Photocopiable sheet 6.4

Barrier game

From *The Crazy Collector* by Diana Hendry, published by Barrington Stoke.

Understanding Different Points of View

Photocopiable sheet 6.5

[1] Use this strategy throughout the day.

Describe the point of view of other people.

'You used the computer last lesson. Matthew hasn't had a turn and wants to write his story. What could you do to help Matthew?'

[2] Help the child complete the 'Favourites' questionnaire on page 137.

[3] Ask the child to interview another person using the 'Favourites' questionnaire.

[4] Talk about which answers are the same and which are different.

Variation 1

[1] Give the child a character.

[2] Other children interview the child who has to respond from the viewpoint of that character.

Variation 2

[1] Cut out pictures from newspapers, magazines or books.

[2] Get the child to fill in speech, feeling and thought bubbles for the different people shown.

Cont'd

Variation 3

1 Draw 'difficult' situations from the child's own experience.

2 Draw events out in sequence. Ask the child 'what happened first?', 'then what happened?', etc. Ask him 'how did it end?'.

3 Ask the child to help fill in speech bubbles for different people involved in the situation. Keep the words and pictures simple.

4 Ask the child to add feeling and thought bubbles for different people. Accept the child's ideas and make alternative suggestions. Show the child that other people may actually have different feelings and thoughts.

For example, *'Maybe Peter was actually thinking "I like Sam. I want him to have different friends as well as me." I'll write that in a thought bubble.'*

5 When the sequence is finished, ask the child to summarise the words and drawings.

6 Help the child think of different solutions to use if a similar situation happens again. What would the child do differently? How would his words, feelings and thoughts be different?

7 Draw or write the solutions for the child. Use these to 'rehearse' situations that he may encounter.

Cont'd

Favourites questionnaire

Where I live:
_____
_____

The people in my family:
_____
_____
_____

What I like to eat:
_____
_____

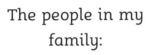

The sports I like:
_____
_____
_____
_____
_____

I get up at: _____
I go to bed at: _____

What I like at school:
_____
_____
_____

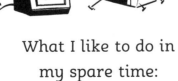

What I like to do in my spare time:
_____
_____
_____

My pets are:
_____
_____
_____

Joining in with Others

Photocopiable sheet 6.6

Use these strategies throughout the day.

- Teach the child to wait until someone has finished before he or she starts to speak. This will reduce interruptions.

- Have a signal to show the child when to join in the conversation.

- Teach the child how to share class equipment and play material, e.g. handing out one pencil to each child.

- Change jobs within the classroom. This will help the child take on different roles.

Variation 1

1. Select a game which can be used for turn taking (lotto, completing a puzzle, snakes and ladders).

2. Talk about whose turn is next and prompt the child to wait.

   For example, *'It's Emma's turn now. Good waiting Tom.'*

3. Make turns clearer, by using an object to pass to the next person who has the next turn.

   For example, *If completing a puzzle, pass on the box containing the puzzle pieces.*

4. Ask the child to say whose turn is next.

Cont'd

Variation 2

[1] Make turns in conversation clear by using an object, such as a beanbag. (A large, light ball can work in place of a small beanbag and can be thrown between speakers.)

[2] The person holding the beanbag may speak.

Variation 3

[1] Role play stories from books. Show the child how to take on the role of different characters.

Variation 4

[1] Describe group 'problems'.

'Someone calls you a nasty name in the playground.'

[2] Suggest different solutions.

'Would you hit them, say a nasty name back, ignore them or tell an adult?'

[3] Ask the child to choose the best solution and give a reason.

[4] Role play the best solution in a group.

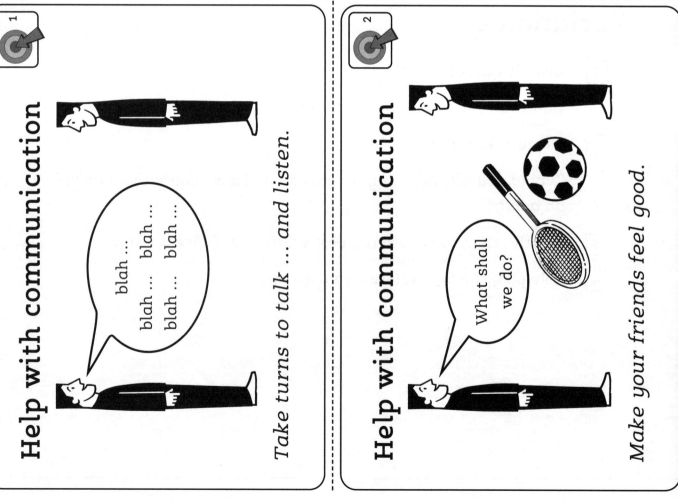

7 Different points of view

Listen to what people say – think about their thoughts and feelings.

8 Joining in with others

To enjoy playtime I can …

- play alone
- sit and watch
- find a friend
- ask to join in

5 Facial expressions

 Happy

Cross

Sad

Calm

Watch people's eyes and mouths – how do they feel?

6 Help the listener understand

"Choose words carefully …"

"… to make me undertand better."

6 Communication Listening and Understanding in Primary Schools © J Reilly & S Murray 2004

139

Glossary

Alliteration – where words in a phrase begin with the same sound or sounds, e.g. 'six sizzling sausages', 'great green grasshoppers'.

Attention – the ability to knowingly focus on an activity, by listening or looking.

Attention Deficit Hyperactivity Disorder – a developmental disorder leading to difficulties sustaining attention, controlling impulsivity and controlling motor activity.

Autistic Spectrum Disorder – a developmental disorder affecting communication, social interaction and imagination. Repetitive behaviours, obsessions and sensory problems may also be present.

Blends – two or more consonants together in a word: *tr, str*.

Blend together – to put together the sounds that make up a word: *s-t-o-p = stop*.

Communication – a two-way process in which two or more people share information, ideas or feelings. It also involves knowing how to listen, watch and wait.

Concept – a combination of ideas, words and images which is broader than single words, e.g. concept 'big' includes all the ideas of the words huge, large, enormous, older, whale, elephant, forest, universe.

Context – the situation to which the information belongs, or refers.

Conversation – turns at talking involving a speaker and listener.

Details – separate pieces of information from the main idea.

Discrimination (auditory) – the ability to hear differences between sounds and words.

Distractions – things which impinge on a child's ability to listen and attend.

Dyslexia – a specific difficulty affecting the learning of reading, spelling and/or writing.

Dyspraxia (Developmental Co-ordination Disorder) – difficulties planning and co-ordinating movements often associated with language, sensory perception and thought.

Inference – looking for meaning beyond the actual information given (reading between the lines).

Learning style – a child's preferred and most effective way of learning.

Listening – the skill of paying attention to information that we hear.

Main idea – separate details or pieces of information connected together as a whole.

Memory – sorts and stores information and organises it for future use.

- **short-term memory** – used to store a limited amount of information for a few seconds.
- **working memory** – used to store one piece of information while working on another piece of the problem.
- **long-term memory** – used to store information for long periods so that it can be retrieved later.

Mind Map™ – a way of recording and organising information about a topic or idea. It shows the relationship between the different aspects of the topic in a colourful way using single words, pictures and symbols. Developed by Tony Buzan.

Morphology – the structure of the word – word beginnings or endings attached to the root word which convey additional meaning about a word, e.g. cat**s**, love**ly**, **un**well.

Multisensory – involving all the senses, e.g. seeing, doing, hearing.

Non-verbal communication – communication that includes facial expression and gesture.

Onsets – the part of the word or syllable which is the first consonant or consonant blend: **t**op, **st**amp.

Phonological awareness – the skill of being aware of sounds within words.

Receptive language – the process by which a listener makes sense of what is heard. Also called understanding.

Rime – the last vowel and consonant or consonant blend in a word or syllable: h*at*, cl*amp*.

Rhyme – words that share the same sounds at the end, usually the last vowel and all sounds after it, e.g. *tray*, *day*.

Sound – what we hear.

Syllable – the beats of the word. The syllable usually contains a vowel.

Topic of conversation – what people are talking about.

Understanding – the process by which a listener makes sense of what is heard, sometimes called 'receptive language'.

Visualisation – turning information and ideas into pictures in the head.

Vocabulary – individual words, usually relating to nouns, verbs, adjectives and adverbs.

Word webs – a way of showing how words are connected around a main concept.

References

Attwood, T. (1998) *Asperger's Syndrome*. Jessica Kingsley Publishers, London.

Bell, N. (1991) *Visualizing and Verbalizing for Language Comprehension and Thinking*. Gander Educational Publishing, San Luis Obispo, California. Available from Winslow, Goyt Side Road, Chesterfield, Derbyshire, S40 2PH.

Fisher, R. (1995) *Teaching Children to Learn*. Stanley Thornes (Publishers) Ltd., Cheltenham.

Fisher, R. (1995) *Teaching Children to Think*. Stanley Thornes (Publishers) Ltd., Cheltenham.

Gerland, G. (1997) *A Real Person. Life on the Outside*. Souvenir Press, London.

Gray, C. (1994) *Comic Strip Conversations*. Future Horizons Inc., Arlington, Texas.

Gray, C. (2002) *My Social Stories Book*. Jessica Kingsley Publishers, London.

Johnson, M. (2001) *Functional Language in the Classroom (and at Home). A Handbook for Children with Communication Difficulties*. Department of Psychology and Speech Pathology, The Manchester Metropolitan University, Manchester.

Levine, M. (1994) *Educational Care. A System for Understanding and Helping Children with Learning Problems at Home and in School*. Educators Publishing Service, Inc., Cambridge, Massachusetts.

Mosley, J. (1998) *Quality Circle Time*. LDA, Cambridge.

Smith, A. and Call, N. (2001) *The ALPS Approach, Resource Book*. Network Educational Press Ltd., Stafford.

Useful Resources and Suppliers

Listening and Attention

Listen, Think and Do. LDA, Duke Street, Wisbech, Cambridge PE13 2AE Tel: 01945 463441. www.LDAlearning.com

S. Edwards, *Speaking and Listening for All*. David Fulton Publishers, London.

Phonological Awareness

Syllabification, Prefixes and Suffixes. Smart Kids (UK), 169B Main Street, New Greenham Park, Thatcham, Berkshire RG45 6HN. Tel: 01635 44037

Gorrie and Parkinson, *Phonological Awareness Procedure*, Stass Publications, 44 North Road, Ponteland, Northumberland NE20 9UR. Tel: 01661 822316

Memory

T. Buzan, *Use your Head*. BBC Books (1995).

T. Buzan, *Mind Maps for Kids – The Shortcut to Success at School*. Thorsons – HarperCollins, London (2003).

J. Brisow, P. Cowley and B. Danes, *Memory and Learning: A Practical Guide for Teachers*. David Fulton Publishers, London (1999).

Jane Mitchell, *Enhancing the Teaching of Memory using Memory Bricks*. CALSC – Communication and Learning Skills Centre, 131 Holmfield Park, Sutton, Surrey SM1 2DY Tel: 0208 642 4663. www.calsc.co.uk

Vocabulary and Concepts

Nanci Bell, *Visualising and Verbalising for Language, Comprehension and Thinking*. Winslow, Goyt Side Road,

Chesterfield, Derbyshire S40 2PH Tel: 0845 921 1777.
www.winslow-press.co.uk

Nanci Bell and Phyllis Lindamood, *Vanilla Vocabulary*. Winslow, Goyt Side Road, Chesterfield, Derbyshire S40 2PH Tel: 0845 921 1777. www.winslow-press.co.uk

Understanding

Looking and Thinking Books, Learning Materials Ltd. Dixon Street, Monmore Green, Wolverhampton, WV2 2BX. Tel: 01902 454026 www.learningmaterials.co.uk

Nanci Bell, *Visualizing and Verbalizing Stories*. Winslow, Goyt Side Road, Chesterfield, Derbyshire S40 2PH Tel: 0845 921 1777. www.winslow-press.co.uk

Ask and Answer Cards. Super Duper Publications, Taskmaster Ltd, Morris Road, Leicester LE2 6BR Tel: 0116 270 4286. www.taskmasteronline.co.uk

Eva Hoffman, *Introducing Children to Mind Mapping*. The Anglo American Book Company Ltd., Crown Buildings, Bancyfelin, Carmarthen, Wales SA33 4ZZ.
Tel: 01267 211880 www.anglo-american.co.uk

Communication

Talking About ... Friends, Black Sheep Press.

Talking About ... School, Black Sheep Press.

Emotions and Facial Expressions, Black Sheep Press.

Speech Bubbles, Black Sheep Press, 67 Middleton, Cowling, Keighley, W. Yorks, BD22 0DQ. Tel: 01535 631 346. www.blacksheeppress.co.uk

Emotions Pack For Kids, Winslow, Goyt Side Road, Chesterfield, Derbyshire, S40 2PH. Tel: 0845 921 1777. www.winslow-press.co.uk

Let's Mime, Winslow, Goyt Side Road, Chesterfield, Derbyshire, S40 2PH. Tel: 0845 921 1777.

Oral Language, Prim-Ed Publishing-UK, P.O. Box 2840, Coventry, CV6 5ZY. Tel: 0870 876 0151. www.prim-ed.com

Index

Attention,
    complex, 35
    development of, 25–26
    listening and, 10–11, 24

Barrier game, 132
Best practice, 22
    classroom, 23
    teacher, 22

Checklists,
    choosing which one to use, 9
    using the, 3, 10
Child strategies,
    listening, 29
Classroom,
    ideal, 23
Communication, 20, 114, 115–116
    checklist, 21
    child strategies, 119–120
    different uses of language, 114–115
    help with, 117–119, 119–120
    talking and learning, 115
    teacher strategies, 117–118
    understanding other people, 114
Conversation,
    barrier game, 132
    changing topic, 121–122
    different points of view, understanding, 133–134
    favourites questionnaire, 135
    helping the listener understand, 130–131
    joining in with others, 136–137
    sticking to topic of, 121–122
    taking turns, 33
    target cards, 138–139

Daily routine, 67
Days of the week, 68, 69
Diagnosis, 3
Distractions,
    strategies for avoiding, 37

Events at the weekend, 71
Everyday expressions, 91

Facial expression and gesture, 128–129
Feelings,
    facial expression and gesture, 128–129
    understanding and controlling, 123–127
Focus,
    helping children, 37
Friends,
    making, 2

Homophones, 87–88

Inference, 108–109
Information,
    gathering, 62
    organising, 79
    remembering, 63
    sorting and storing, 62–63

Learning,
    process of, 6
    styles, 64–65
    top tips for, 7
Links, organising and making, 90
Listening,
    attention and, 10–11

choosing what to listen to, 1–2
classroom, in the, 24
complex, 35
development of, 25–26
difficulties, 2
emotional factors in, 26
help with, 27–28, 29
memory and, 25
skills, 24
    areas involved in, 4–5
target cards, 38
teacher strategies, 27-28
walk, 32

Maths, language of, 80
Memory, 60
    case study, 14
    checklist, 15
    child strategies, 66
    class discussion, 73–74
    daily routine and, 67
    days of the week, 68, 69
    development of, 63
    events at the weekend, 71
    help with, 64–66
    information,
        gathering, 62
        remembering, 63
        sorting and storing, 62–63
    listening and, 25
    months of the year, 68, 70
    story, remembers details from, 73–74
    strategy for remembering, 75
    target cards, 76–77
    teacher strategies, 64–65
    three kinds of, 60–61
    three part sequence, 72
    three parts to, 61
Mind map, 111
Months of the year, 68, 70

Noise,
    ignoring, 32

On task,
    keeping, 31

Phonological awareness, 12, 39
    alliteration, 49-50
    checklist, 13
    child strategies, 43
    help with, 41–42, 43
    individual sounds in words, 51–52
    prefixes in speech, 53
    reading and, 40
    rhyming words, 47–49
    similar sounds, 54–55
    speech and, 40
    suffixes in speech, 53
    syllables, 44–46
    target cards, 56–59
    teacher strategies, 41–42
Prefixes in speech, 53

Quotes, 8

Resources, 144–145
Rhyming words, 47–48

Sounds,
    discriminating, 28
    locating, 25
Story,
    listening to a, 30
Suffixes in speech, 53
Syllables, 44–46

Taking turns, 33
Target cards, 4
Teacher,
    qualities of ideal, 22
    strategies, 27–28
Traffic light system, 100

Understanding, 94
    applying previous learning, 110
    case study, 18
    checklist, 19
    child strategies, 99–100
    defining, 94
    difficulties with, 95
    help with, 96–98, 99–100
    inference, 108–109
    learning and, 94
    main ideas, 104–105
    mind map, 111
    questions, 101–103
    skill areas involved in, 4–5
    target cards, 112–113
    teacher strategies, 96–98
    traffic light system, 100
    visualisation, 106–107

Visualisation, 106–107
Vocabulary,
    accuracy in use, 89
    checklist, 17
    child strategies, 83–84
    concepts and, 16–17, 78, 86
    everyday expressions, 91
    help with, 81–82, 83–84
    homophones, 87–88
    information, organising, 79
    learning, 85
    maths, language of, 80
    organising and making links, 90
    target cards, 92–93
    teacher strategies, 81–82

Acknowlegements

The publishers would like to thank the following for permission to use their copyright material. It is the belief of both the publishers and the authors that every effort has been made to trace copyright holders. However, should there be any omissions in this respect, we apologise and on receipt of relevant information, agree to make the appropriate acknowledgements in future editions.

Pictures

Kirstin Holbrow from 'The Genie' by Mary Hooper, by permission of the publisher (1999); Kirstin Holbrow from 'Crazy Collector' by Diana Hendry, by permission of the publisher (2001).

Text

Gunilla Gerland from 'Life on the Outside', by permission of Souvenir Press Ltd., London (1997); Jeremy Strong from 'Mad Iris', by permission of the publisher (2002); Robert Fisher from 'Teaching Children to Learn', by permission of Nelson Thornes Ltd., Cheltenham (1995); Joseph O'Connor and Ian McDermott from 'NLP' by permission of HarperCollins, London (2001); Alistair Smith and Nicola Call from 'The ALPS Approach Resource Book: accelerated learning in primary schools', by permission of Network Educational Press, Stafford (2001).